The Book of Hope, An Anthology
31 True Stories
from Real People
Who Didn't Give Up

Edited by Krysta Gibson

Silver Owl Publications, Monroe, WA

Books by Krysta Gibson:
    Anything is Possible
    Comments on Leading the Spiritual Life
    22 Steps to Success
    Business Success for Body, Mind, & Spirit
    How to Get Your Article Printed in a Magazine or Newspaper
    22 Pasos Hacia El Exito (en Español)
    Las Herramientas del Emprendedor (en Español)

Krysta has a weekly television show called Keeping It Real at ShareWisdom.tv

Courses, guided meditations, and self-talk MP3s can be found at www.krystagibson.com

Book cover and book design by Rhonda Dicksion www.indigodog.com

Tradepaper ISBN 978-1-879375-05-5
EBook ISBN: 978-1-879375-06-2

First Printing March 2017
Printed in the United States of America
Silver Owl Publications is a women owned and operated company.

Dedication

Dedicated to my sister, Kitti Lindusky.

Contents

Introduction

Is there anyone who has not lost hope at some point in their lives? Who hasn't had life throw roadblocks in the way? Who hasn't lost loved ones, had financial disasters, career or health challenges? And who can say they have always handled these situations with grace and honor?

In this priceless collection of true stories experienced by everyday people like you and me, readers get to share in the angst, the grief, the frustration and fears of the writers. And then we get to experience how these brave souls transformed their situations and benefited from them.

While preparing this book for you, I have had the honor of reading these stories more than once. Each time, my heart was touched by the depth of vulnerability these writers were willing to experience. Sometimes while reading them, I had to stop, breathe, and have a cup of tea. Sometimes, it was almost too much to read in one sitting.

What struck me deeply is the resiliency of the human spirit. Even when faced with destitution or total abandonment by one's own family, these folks found their way out of their personal dark woods and back into the world of light and hope.

This collection of stories proves there is always hope no matter how negative our situation might be. It is my fervent wish that you, the reader, will feel inspired and encouraged as you read *The Book of Hope*. Please share these stories with as many people as you can, especially those who you know are suffering similar fates.

Sometimes, just knowing someone else has walked your path opens the doors and windows so new ideas and solutions can flow.

Blessings to all,
Krysta Gibson
March 2017

Hope Regained at Christmastime

by Marybeth Mitcham

Most people equate the winter holiday season to joy and laughter, memory-making and surprises; but for some, it can be the most devastating time of the year. Despite overwhelming hardships, those pain-filled holiday seasons can actually become the best ones yet. Although I have been blessed with many wonderful memories of glorious holidays over the years, the most memorable holiday of all fell during one of the hardest years of my life; one in which I felt that I had lost all hope.

It wasn't enough that unexpectedly I had been laid-off from my job as a result of the economic recession, but both household cars ended up needing massively expensive repairs, our home furnace died, and other several important appliances decided to follow suit. Because that wouldn't have been enough just by itself, our precious store of firewood that would have ensured that our home could have been heated during the harsh northern winter (despite the nonfunctional furnace) was carried away by a freak flash flood that tore through our property, not once, but twice; the second time, after neighbors had blessed us with enough firewood to replace the first amount that had been lost during that first freak flood.

Our tank of propane to run our kitchen stove and water heater was almost empty, and we did not have the money to refill it. Despite pouring over local newspaper help-wanted ads, spending countless hours every day looking online for job openings, and asking friends and neighbors if they knew of any work opportunities, none presented themselves. Our regular monthly bills were piling up, and our bank account was empty.

The final blow came a few weeks before Christmas when some medical tests that had been performed on me came back with an initial probable diagnosis of cancer.

It was Christmastime.

We had no money for necessities.

Our cupboards were almost bare.

Our children sorely needed winter clothing that we could not afford to purchase.

We had no way to fix the items that needed fixing.

We had no means by which to keep the house warm that winter.

We had no money with which to buy presents for our children.

Despite the apparent hopelessness of the situation, my husband continued to remind me that provision had always come to us, and that if we did our part to continue to work and do all that we could, we might see a Christmas miracle.

I have to admit that I had no such hope. I actually could not remember feeling that hopeless ever before; not when our unborn child was diagnosed with a severe congenital deformity, not when another child was diagnosed with autism, not even when my husband was deployed overseas as an infantryman during war. Despite those hardships, I had always still felt hope.

Despite my hopelessness, my husband continued to work as hard as he could, quietly going without food, sleep, or even a bed at night, so that he could provide for his family. I worked hard to stretch every penny, and tried my best to at least act like I had hope for my children's sake.

Even though presents under the Christmas tree were the least of our worries, and there was obviously no extra money that year for presents, I wanted my children to still have a fun holiday season. Remembering how my mother had made my childhood holidays seem magical despite our family's extreme poverty, I decided to attempt to do something similar with my children.

I sat my children down and told them that rather than focusing on presents that year, we would hold a game. The game would be a combination of a stealthy purchase made for their sibling's present combined with a Christmas-morning search for those presents. The rules of the game were simple: each child was to be given $5. With that $5, they would have to find and then purchase a gift for their sibling, all while their sibling was doing the same thing, in the same store. The goal of the game was not only to purchase a gift that would be enjoyed by the other person, but to do so without the other person finding out what was purchased.

That game idea was a huge hit with my children, and became my turning point from hopelessness to hope.

I wish that I could have bottled up the giggles that rang in the store the day that we had our Stealthy Christmas Gift Purchase Game. My children darted from aisle to aisle, trying to elicit the workers in the store to assist them in distracting their sibling so that they could successfully make their purchase in secret. The entire store got involved in my children's efforts, each person working to make sure that my children had a fantastic time. At the end of the game, each child held their prize, carefully wrapped by the cashiers in multiple layers of plastic bags so that the hidden treasure would not be seen by their sibling.

When we got home from the store, my children carefully wrapped the gifts, and then gave them to me for safekeeping until Christmas morning. As I helped my youngest child wrap his sister's gift in newspaper, I noticed an ad in the paper, requesting heartening stories about keeping the Christmas spirit alive. As my children's laughter and obvious delight in the game had caused me to feel something that I had not felt in months — joy and hope — I wanted to share that knowledge with others who might be struggling. So, I quickly drafted an email, describing the game — the reason behind it as well as the joy that it brought — and then went back to helping my son finish wrapping his present.

Even though I was still worried about how we would make it, the hope that I felt at that moment made all of the difference.

And that was just the beginning. Little did I know how much that simple email would change things.

A few minutes later, I received an email from one of the editors of the newspaper, asking for more details about my family's choice to still choose joy in the Christmas season, despite our challenging situations. Still thinking that it might help someone else, I wrote back a slightly longer email that briefly described the events of the past year as well as our family's choices to celebrate the season.

As soon as I sent that email, the phone rang.

It was my husband.

His company had just notified him that overtime would be offered to him the following week if he wanted it, despite the fact that it had not been available to anyone in almost 10 years. They had noticed his hard work and excellent work ethic, and wanted him to be the one that was able to get the extra time.

To say that I cried tears of joy would be an understatement.

Right after I hung the phone up, it rang again.

It was the doctor's office. The tests were negative. I was cancer-free.

I didn't think that it could get any better, but it did.

The next day, the newspaper ran a lead article about my family's positive outlook, in spite of our circumstances. Despite my extreme embarrassment at being featured in that way, the article led to an incredible amount of positive feedback from the community, as many people vocalized their appreciation at being reminded about the true meaning of the holidays. People also showed their appreciation by blessing us with gifts: money that exactly covered the cost of firewood, propane, the vehicle repairs, and the necessary appliance repairs, gift cards that allowed us to purchase the winter clothing and boots that our children needed, as well as purchase food and other necessities that we had just run out of, and even home-baked goodies to cheer us up.

That Christmas morning, as our children scoured the house to find their preciously-bought present, chosen and secured by their sibling during the Stealthy Christmas Gift Purchase Game, my husband and I overflowed with joy, for we knew that, regardless of our income, we had what was truly important.

Friends.

Community.

Family.

What it took for hope to be regained was a shift in my focus, choosing to make the most of what we had been blessed with — and fully enjoy it — rather than on what we were missing.

That is a lesson that I will never forget, and am so very grateful that I had the opportunity to learn.

There is always hope.

You just need to where to look for it.

My Diagnosis

by A.C. Graham

I still remember that day as if it were yesterday. It was approximately a week after my twenty-third birthday. I considered myself fresh out of college even though by then I had been working for more than a year. I recalled waking up one morning with some red spots on my body and a fever that lasted for a day, but I did not panic at all. After all, everything was fine after two days had passed. I attributed my tiredness to the fever and forgot all about it.

About a month later, I went to my doctor for my routine check-up. I figured that the results would be similar to the ones that I had been diagnosed with in the past. However, the doctor called me personally two days later. I began to fear for the worst. My mom had passed away slightly less than four years prior from a complication of breast and liver cancer. I thought that I might be diagnosed with something similar.

When I finally got to the doctor's office, he gestured at the seat next to him with a grim expression on his face. I honestly could not recall everything that occurred or every sensation and thought that I experienced as I waited for him to search for my health results. I did remember that my heart had been thumping like mad and the cold sweat was breaking out all over my body. Once he was seated on his chair, he pushed the slip of paper towards me and pointed at a particular word.

I could not feel or think about anything after that. I had been diagnosed with an HIV-positive result.

There was a weird numbness all over me as if I was looking at the whole situation through the eyes of someone else. The doctor gave me a few minutes for the reality to sink in before going into a long-winded explanation of what I should be doing next. There was the blood-check for my CD4 count and a counseling session immediately after.

(A CD4 count is a lab test that measures the number of CD4 T lymphocytes — CD4 cells — in a sample of your blood. In people with HIV, it is the most important laboratory indicator of how well your immune system is working and the strongest predictor of HIV progression.) Nothing had truly registered in my mind though.

I went through the next few days in this strange state of consciousness. It was as if everything was fine. There was no catastrophic incident happening all around me, but I had been so lost and frightened about my future that, even if there was a disaster right next to me, I would probably end up ignoring it. I was uncertain if I had accepted my status then, but I withdrew into myself for the duration.

I did not know who I should be confiding to. I had been very close to my mom prior to her passing. She had been the only person whom I could trust wholly and implicitly. However, even in that state of mind, I had realized that I needed to talk to somebody. The counselor had been clinical and professional, and she had given me a ton of resources to assist me, but it really did not make it any better.

I somehow convinced myself to open up to my sister. I was torn between telling her the truth and keeping my mouth shut about it. There was no surefire guarantee that anyone would be able to accept another person's HIV-positive status regardless of one's relation to the other party.

Nonetheless, my sister and I eventually found a quiet spot somewhere in the house. I told her about my diagnosis, showing her the results and all the advice that I had been given by the doctor and the counselor.

There were plenty of tears between the two of us. To say that it was one of the most difficult conversations I ever had was a gross understatement. I did implore her to keep my status to herself for the time being. I was not ready to tell anyone else. Truth be told, I had barely accepted it myself.

The next few weeks were a weird mix of self-acceptance and self-loathing. I did go through my usual routines every day, but I was not completely myself. I was not aware of many things that were happening during that particular period of time. There were days when I thought that I had come to terms with the reality of my life. Then, there would be those days when I had ended up crying myself to sleep. There were even some evenings when either I could not sleep at all or I would be having a restless sleeping pattern, waking up every hour or so for no apparent reason.

I wish that I had a miraculous breakthrough or a magical way of dealing with the lingering sense of hopelessness, but sadly I didn't. I started looking at life differently. The logical part of me had known that the advancement in medical technology meant that being HIV-positive was not the death sentence that it once was, but I was probably going through a depression of sorts.

During these weird times, I had thought about my mom and her two-year battle with cancer. It was morbid and insane, but I was probably too dejected to sensor my thoughts and feelings. Honestly, I did not know how I would ever get back up and live my life all over again because that was the essence of the diagnosis for me personally. My life was not the same anymore.

I had dreamed about having a good relationship and growing old together, but I knew that most people would be too afraid to get close to someone of my status. At that time, it felt like my life was over. I could not see through the fog of melancholy that I had been experiencing. Then again, I probably refused to find the silver lining. Instead, I had chosen to be dispirited, allowing myself to be pulled by the tide rather than fighting against it.

I could not pour my heart out to my sister too often. I felt horrible about unloading all of my concerns onto her. It would be unfair. At that time, I had not divulged my status to my parents or to the rest of my siblings. I was too scared of their reactions. It was not an easy topic to broach. I ended up bottling everything inside me. There were days when it seemed as if I would explode from the inside out.

I was getting more sullen as the days passed by, but I did not have a good solution. All I knew then was that I desperately needed an outlet to release all of my pent-up frustrations. For some obscure reason, I started to tidy up all of my things. That was when it hit me. I had been packing up left and right when I discovered my old diaries. I had quite a few of them.

When I was much younger, I had found that writing in my diaries was a good way to relieve my volatile feelings. I had written many things on those pages. That had been a very therapeutic way of dealing with my adolescent fears. It was then that I decided to pick up where I had left off.

Writing in a diary had been somewhat similar to riding a bicycle. I was initially rather stiff and awkward in my writing because it had been a while since I last wrote anything in a diary. However, I soon got the hang of it. The words flowed much more smoothly the more often I poured out all of my fears and concerns onto the blank pages. It came to a point where I eventually rediscovered my passion for life. Gradually, I started listening to music again to soothe my inner turmoil. I even wrote poetry on and off, especially when the muse hit me.

I was not fully healed, though. After all, I had held back from informing my parents and siblings, and I truly wanted them to know. I pondered over it for several months, going back and forth between telling them and otherwise. In the meantime, writing and music remained the main outlets where I could simply live in the moment. My desire to live more healthily led me to purchase natural herbs and tons of multivitamins. I also added yoga and Pilates to my routine instead of only relying on cardiovascular exercises to keep myself as healthy as I possibly could.

When I finally talked to my parents and siblings, they took it rather well. They required a little time to absorb the reality of my diagnosis, but the situation was better than I expected. There was no consequential drama that I had to endure. There were definitely plenty of tears all around, but their acceptance pushed me to live my life and face the crisis head-on.

This openness has helped me face my life with more courage. I have discovered new passions and a more positive outlook towards life in general. I have survived for almost eleven years now, and I will not be slowing down anytime soon. In fact, I have been blessed with somebody who is willing to accept my status and love me regardless of it. We celebrated our four-year anniversary in January 2017. It has been a long road since my diagnosis and there are times when I wonder what my life would be like if I had not been infected, but those moments are getting fewer and rarer. I have vowed to live my life the best way I know how and keep the fire of hope burning brightly inside me.

I am a survivor.

Hope Comes in Paper Bags

by Trisha Mahi

When we are babies, we hope that our mothers will come and pick us up when we cry. We hope that somebody will change our wet diaper, and we hope that somebody feeds us.

When we are children, we hope that everybody is nice to us at school. We hope that we get good grades. We hope that nobody notices how many cookies are gone. We hope that Santa will give us a pass and bring us presents regardless of how we behaved from January to November.

When we get a little older we hope that somebody takes us to the prom. We hope we get the right job and that we find the right partner in love. We have some fits and starts and mistakes and heartbreaks but vigorous youth sustains and gets us through these years.

When we are adults, hope takes on a different meaning because we feel that we have control over situations. It's really nice to think that we are in charge, but we would be so incredibly wrong. Just about the time that we have reached our pinnacle of mastery in this world there comes a crash.

This story is about the most horrible, hopeless days of my life in which the currency of hope flew out of my life in less than 24 hours.

That weekday dawned with a great deal of pain in my back. However, being a good sport and a workaholic, I went to my volunteer gig and worked from six am to noon. I didn't want to let my colleagues down.

Privately I knew that once I got home that afternoon I would enjoy the pain medication I take, as Matt Damon did in the movie, *Martian*, relishing scraping Vicodin on his potato when he ran out of ketchup.

When I got home at about 1 o'clock, I took the pain pill and lay back on my bed waiting for the magic of pain relief. I had just drifted off into that in-between state of sleep where pain tapers off into relief.

The dog started barking around 2 o'clock and I heard pounding on my front door. There was a man on my porch with a paper with masking tape on it. He was putting up a notice saying that my house was being foreclosed on. My roommate panicked and immediately started packing her bags. My reassurances that this was a mistake flew over her head.

This man was so thorough in his work that he even put a foreclosure sign on one of my farm's outbuildings. I guess he figured the termites or barn rats might want to relocate as well.

I tried to explain to the man (who wasn't listening) that I had obtained a mortgage modification and that I was just waiting to hear my new payment amount. The man totally ignored my words and continued reciting his speech, which I'm sure he had memorized. I think he was happy I wasn't a big guy ready to pound him into the ground.

The source of my foreclosure problem was my misplaced trust. I foolishly invested money in a business, and that money was consumed in the form of vodka by my talented but shiftless partner. This was the year of the failing banks, bailouts, and total chaos. I was adrift in the financial storm myself.

So I sat in my living room half dopey from the medicine. I had given-up making pleas to my roommate that all was going to be well. And, frankly, I was worried that something had gone wrong with my mortgage modification and I was going to join the ranks of the homeless. I deeply feared that I was in trouble, but it was too late in the day to call the bank to find out if this was all just an error.

I went to bed that night still bleary from the medication. Possibly the haze was God's gift. The enormity of losing my home and my roommate to my failing business along with my sore back was just too much. I had given up hope, but at least things couldn't get worse.

But they did.

The phone jangled me awake around two in the morning. I fumbled for the phone and heard my cousin on the other end of the line speaking as fast as an auctioneer. She said, "Mom's died... Think she had a heart attack...Dad is at the hospital alone and I'm getting the kids ready to go to the hospital... Please go sit with him since he is alone with Mom."

The vision of my brother-in-law sitting alone with his beloved wife, my sister, in the cold, concrete halls in the bowels of the hospital was just too much. I tossed on wrinkled clothes and sped down the highway, the only car for miles. Save for my headlights, this was a pitch black night.

I pulled into a parking place in the emergency area of the hospital. The scene was just as cold and uncomfortable as my imagination had warned me. My brother-in-law, an esteemed doctor in this little community, sat slumped on a folding chair in a room next to the morgue, staring at the face of my sister who looked like she was sleeping. She had just died of a heart attack at home, so she still had a flush of life in her face.

It ran through my mind that the hospital could have found a less harsh place for this man to spend these last moments with his wife. Everything was gray and white. The only color I noticed was the purple glow of her wedding ring still on her hand.

I am not sure if he and I spoke. I had entered that automaton-like functioning-without- thinking phase that we go into when we see something that our minds cannot take in. My sister was the one person who I could always call for advice or just company. She was my closest friend, too.

Thirty minutes later the room erupted in noise as my cousin and her children came tumbling into the room with my cousin shushing the throng. Everyone looked slightly disheveled and sleepy and we were all in a state of shock. My sister was the glue that had kept all of us together. She was the first to tell us when we were doing something wrong and praise us if we did well. We all loved her.

I looked around the room and wondered how the hell we were going to carry on? From the look on my brother-in-law's face, I felt that he had already left us and the light had gone out of the family.

I am from an Eastern European background — mostly Jewish — and if you know us then you know our solution for any problem is food. I asked my cousin's eldest son if he would drive me to the 24-hour McDonald's. I bought maybe $40 worth of assorted breakfast sandwiches.

We brought the steaming paper bags back in to the room where my sister was laid out under a sheet. We all found creaky folding chairs and sat there around her dead body eating McDonald's. She was in the very center, with maybe ten of us surrounding her, all of us with food in our hands.

The first person to laugh was my cousin. She said "It looks like Mom is going to sit up and ask for a bite." It did look like any moment she would sit up and ask where hers was, but I was too polite to say so. I was happy my cousin did.

Each of us in turn started laughing quietly and realizing a little bit of McDonald's had glued us together into family again instead of lonely individuals traveling the grief road alone. My cousin's sense of humor raised us up.

Though we would all have our private bouts of grief, at that moment we had hope. It may sound silly to read but biting into a sausage Mc-Muffin, enjoying a literal last meal with my sister, was in a macabre way fun. We had gone from being a room full of individuals alone in their grief to a family starting to recover together. Hope lives in all of us; it just sometimes needs to be nourished.

I went home and tore the foreclosure sign off my house and outbuilding, and watched the sun rise over Mauna Loa. There was sadness for the passing of my sister, but I had a newfound knowledge that we are a strong family and there was nothing we couldn't face together.

Miracles happen. I did keep my house and am still happily living in it. And yes, my sister remained dead, but she had been painfully ill for years; perhaps her release from this world was what was best for her.

When her husband remarried, we told the newlyweds, "Mazel tov," and enjoyed the wedding. Families aren't always blood; sometimes family love comes from our friends. Good friends and a loving family is the closest thing to heaven that we have here.

Nobody is immune to grief, money problems, and physical ailments; they just happen. Here are a few of the lessons I learned.

First is to get a tribe of people you can count on and who can count on you. This is an investment that pays better than any other.

Second, just because someone with authority is standing on your doorstep looking official doesn't make them right. I did have a mortgage modification, but their left hand didn't know what their right hand was doing.

Third, be persistent. If you really want something, go after it like a hungry trout jumps for a feather lure! Don't take "no" for an answer. Get real muscle when you are in trouble. My mortgage modification came through, in part, through the diligence of U.S.Senator Daniel K. Inouye's office.

Fourth, when things look bad, a good hot shower and a good night's sleep make everything look better. Remember to eat.

Fifth, pick your partners carefully. My drinking alcoholic business partner broke my heart and took my money, but I own the bad choices I made. Seriously, drinking alcoholics are assholes of the first water; avoid them like Ebola and rattlesnakes.

Finally, enjoy life. When my sister woke up on that last day of her life she didn't know by late night we would be surrounding her dead body munching McDonalds. I hope that day was fun for her and that she saw us having our picnic, and laughed!

Transformed Through Breast Cancer

by Francine L. Billingslea

It was December, 2002. I slowly pulled into my garage, turned my SUV off, and sat a minute. I was tired. Twenty-eight years working for a major auto corporation on the assembly line had taken its toll and these last two years couldn't come fast enough.

Lethargically entering the house, I flopped down on the overstuffed couch and looked around. A wide smile came across my face as thoughts about my job, my home, and my life rapidly ran through my mind. The hard work, the relocation, the new house, the divorce... Yes, it was all worth it. Everything I ever dreamed of, prayed for, and worked for, I now had. I was happier than I've ever been. After years and years of struggling, at the ripe young age of forty-eight, everything had fallen into place. I had finally arrived. Not only that, but in two more years, I could retire and really enjoy the fruits of my labor. I had big plans.

I glanced at the clock, time was flying. I had to shower, change and get to the hairdresser. Christmas was just two days away and I still had a lot to do. Thankful that the plant was closed for a month, as I quickly showered and dressed, I mentally went over my to-do list: Get my hair done today, my manicure and pedicure tomorrow; do some last minute shopping; pack my bag; leave to go to North Carolina to my sister's house bright and early Christmas morning, and while I'm there have a blast like I also do; as soon as I get back make an appointment for my annual mammogram; clean out my closets; then do what really needed to be done and that was to do absolutely nothing but to simply rest and relax until it was time to go back to work.

The holidays quickly came and went, and now it was January 2003. Two weeks into the New Year and yes, I had caught up on my rest and relaxation in-between doing some things around the house. As a matter of fact, I had done everything I said I was going to do and then some; everything except get that dreaded mammogram. With less than two weeks left before having to return back to work, I called and made my appointment.

As the technician pulled and stretched my left breast into position, I told her about my self-diagnosis of arthritis in my shoulder that seemed to be traveling down my arm. She smiled, lied, and said, "I'll be as gentle as I can," as she pressed the plate down as far as she could to tightly hold my throbbing smashed breast in place. Running into a small cubical, she yelled out, "Please be still and hold your breath!" I yelled back, "I can't, the pain is excruciating!" Her reply, "This will only take a minute!" Not wanting it to last any longer, I tearfully bore the pain. When she finally released me from the monster's grip, I almost fell to the floor. Other than the usual discomfort, the right side was effortless.

"Please have a seat in the waiting room and don't get dressed. I'll be back in a few minutes," she said as she hurried out of the room. I sat in a big soft chair that seemed to hug me. Tears ran down my cheeks as the now agonizing pain danced around my breast, across my shoulder and up and down my arm. The technician came back almost an hour later and said, "I'm sorry to inform you, but I'm going to have to do your left side again." This time, the dance was more intense. After, I was led down the hall for a sonogram, then told to come back Monday morning for a biopsy.

The biopsy came back positive. I had stage II breast cancer. A week later, I had a lumpectomy instead of the expected mastectomy. Two weeks later, I started the first round of chemotherapy of which I had to have every twenty-one days for six months and shortly after, radiation would follow.

After the second round of chemo, my hair began to fall out, which was another ruthless sneak attack. I became fatigued and anemic. I lost my appetite, lost weight, and had dark circles around my eyes. I looked like a stick lady with a bowling ball head. I didn't want anyone to see me. I didn't want to go out; not even to the mailbox. Depression played its game. I'd stare in the mirror and didn't know the person who stared back. I felt as if life had blindsided and played some cruel joke on me, lifting me up to the highest high then dropping me to the lowest low. I was angry. I was irate. I was downright pissed-off! I was scared to think about healing or my future because I didn't know if I would be healed, and if that was the case, I didn't even have a future. As hard as I tried, I couldn't find "I cared" anywhere. And as for my plans, the only plan I had that was guaranteed was my funeral. My perfect world had come to an end.

One day, I just got tired of being sick and tired, and depressed. I started thinking about how I struggled and fought to get to where I was and get what I had. I thought about my loving mother, my daughter, my grandchildren, my sister and my companion who, by the way, is now my husband. I had to fight for them. Win or lose, at least try to set an example.

I thought about all I had to live for. I thought about all I had been through before the cancer and I realized I was always a fighter. I was always a survivor because I never gave up and I couldn't now. Something began to rise up within me. It was two things that I always relied on. It was hope and faith that always motivated my strength and determination. I had reached my goals but made the mistake of becoming too complacent. Through the years, I had learned that sometimes it's the hardest struggles that give you your most valuable lessons and blessings. I had forgotten this. Now I was in the hardest struggle of all and my life literally depended on it. There was a reason for this season in my life and I aimed to find out what it was.

I looked in the mirror and yelled, "Okay cancer, you gave me your best shot, now, I'm going to give you mine!" I began to pray like I never prayed before. I began to fight, not like a girl, but like the woman I was and like the woman I wanted to become. I made myself eat when I didn't want to. I drank gallons of water and juice. I walked. I exercised. I reconditioned my mind to think positive thoughts and constantly proclaimed positive affirmations, and even on my worst days. When I looked in the mirror, I didn't see a bald, sick, emaciated person looking back, I visualized a healthy, full-haired, happy person who had been through a test and came out with a testimony. In time, my visualization became reality.

Slowly healing, retired, and totally bored, I laid around disheveled, with my hair pointing to the four corners of the earth, praying that I'd find something to do to occupy my time and mind. Adhering to my daughter's and sister's advice, I invested in a computer which, for the most part, sat in the corner of my room collecting dust.

In 2007, while browsing on my basically unused computer, I came across a contest for breast cancer patients and survivors. Struggling to put years of my journey into the three hundred maximum word count and not being a typist, nor a writer, I pecked out my story, hesitantly submitted it, and forgot all about it. A few weeks later, to my utmost surprise, I was notified that I was a winner. I had found my lesson, my blessing. and my new niche. Soon, everything I ever saw, heard, or experienced became a sentence or a paragraph for a short story. I began to write about everything!

In 2009, I was declared cancer-free, I remarried, and was a published author of seven short stories and counting, never dreaming that six years later, it would be up to forty-two.

It is now 2016. At the ripe young age of 62, I'm happy to report that I am still cancer-free, but my journey isn't over. It'll be a lifetime of medications and doctor visits, but also of prayer, faith, hope, determination and struggles. But I've learned to make lemonade out of life's lemons. I've learned that health, family, and love are more important than material things. I've learned to plan but to leave those plans in our creator's hands and pray that His will be done according to His plan for our lives. I've come to the full understanding and knowledge that our time here on earth is limited, so take each day as it comes and live that day to its fullest, and no matter what that day might bring, be thankful in all things because in all things, there are things to be thankful for.

Yes, my life has been transformed through breast cancer. The character, wisdom, strength, and peace that was built in me — and some of the people I've met who have been on cancer journeys that made mine seem like a day at the beach — is life-changing within itself. It has made me see who I am and what I'm about through writing, encouraging, inspiring, supporting others, and speaking about it.

Breast cancer tried to destroy me and it would have, had I allowed it to. But in reality, it taught me to be more resilient and to always keep hope alive, no matter what we may be going through. Breast cancer offered me chances and changes, a new way of living and thankfully, I took them.

Now, I can honestly say that I have finally arrived. I'm happier now than I've ever been. I now know that I had to get seriously knocked down to get seriously built up. No, I'm not thankful that life threw me a curve ball in the form of breast cancer, but I am thankful, very thankful, that my life has been positively transformed because of it.

Living with an Entity

by Niobe Weaver

I always prided myself as a smart, independent woman, who would never allow herself to get into an abusive relationship. I had ended relationships at the slightest hint of something being off. What I am going to share took that pride and brought me to a place I had never been in my life.

It was 2002, and following the success of my first sound healing workshop, my mentor offered to finance my first CD. He found a local studio and together we went to check it out. We left feeling this was "spirit-driven" and celebrated over Thai food. (A little backstory here. I wasn't a longtime singer/songwriter finally getting to record her first CD. I was a sound healer not really sure what I wanted to produce, but thinking I would create a toning, meditation CD.)

Along came the first day to start the project. The producer in the studio was a seasoned guitar player and recording artist. He picked up his guitar and said, "What do you have for me?" Needless to say, I was nervous and a bit intimidated. It had been twenty-plus years since being around the recording world and singing in a band, but I mustered up my confidence and sang a short song that I had written recently. The next three months were spent discovering music and lyrics that were waiting to be born. I finished with 14 songs. Seven of the melodies were mine and seven were my producer's, and I wrote all the lyrics. I had no idea this was inside me!

You hear about people getting involved doing creative projects, and by the end of the three months, the producer was sparking on me pretty hard and I was enjoying the attention. It had been five years since my partner had died of cancer and I was feeling it was time to allow someone into my life. He certainly had cast his spell. I believed him when he told me he and his girlfriend were going their separate ways. He was so charming, seemingly transparent and honest. We had a lot in common.

He was a widower, had two grown children, was a recovering Catholic, spiritual, and he was so captivated by me. I never had anyone pursue me like this. We had made magic in the studio musically, so it should be that way in relationship right?! Oh, how naïve I was.

We ended the project the first of April. By June, he had moved in with me and my two sons.

The first year was like most first years of a relationship: all warm and fuzzy. Passionate. But there were signs that actually were red flags. I saw them and chose to look the other way. You know the saying, "I walked down the road, I saw a hole in the road and still jumped in." That was me. As that first year ended, he stopped being who I had fallen in love with. Not because he couldn't, it was because he didn't need to be that man. He had what he wanted: a new home, new woman. He could be himself and reveal who he really was.

When the mask of "nice, sweet guy" was ripped off, I was stunned by what I witnessed. That anger, the screaming, the fit-throwing, the alcohol; who is he channeling? His father? He frightened me some, but here is where my pride came into play. I can handle this; he is my mother and father stuff all in one. I can work out my shit and stick with it.

I had never been successful with longevity in relationships. Four years was my track record and I was determined to make this work. My judgement of myself as "a failure in relationships" was a constant tape playing in my head. And quietly, I didn't want to admit to my closest sister friends or my children that I was in major trouble, and that I had picked such a wrong guy. That was my ego not listening to my soul that was yelling at me to flee.

Life quickly became a surreal world of light and dark. I love you's to I'm sorry, would repeat again and again in a bizarre six-week cycle. Drunken rages, sober meanness, and indifference, accompanied by constant daily mind games, became my life. I continued to hide this as my youngest son went on to college and we became an empty nest.

The music of 2002 called and I was guided to start booking us as a music duo in 2005, performing our original music in churches. This would prove to be the only light that was true between us for the next eight years. On the outside, we looked like this amazing spiritual musical couple. If only they knew what was going on behind closed doors, or right before a gig. I felt so out of integrity, a hypocrite, hiding that I had lost control of my life. The thing that I was most determined to not allow to happen in my life had happened.

He had steadily taken over almost everything from how to shop for groceries, who gets the mail, the check book and finances. Any money I made disappeared into supposedly paying bills, but actually was paying for the studio gear and who knows what else. 2004 to 2010 was filled with the death, serious illness, or severe accidents, to family or friends at least one every year. One of my sons went through a terrifying experience, and I am lucky to have him still alive, well, and successful in life. It was like I had opened a deep realm of darkness, and invited it in. I was in a daily spiritual battle; it was exhausting and wearing me down. However, I never lost faith. I knew somehow, some way, I would get out of this relationship. I just didn't know how or when.

Liberation came in 2013. He finally became weary of trying to change me and found someone else. As deeply as this betrayal hurt, at the same time I was grateful to her. I was finally free. Over the weeks of separating our lives, I would learn what narcissistic personality disorder and narcissistic abuse entails. I was absolutely devastated to read my life on a website. Now I finally understood what and who I had been living with. I now saw the entity as I dealt with him. I was physically, emotionally, and mentally drained. My spirit and my spiritual connection was the only thing that held me through all of these years.

I moved to Seattle with $150, an old car, needing surgery, and $48,000 in debt. But I was free! I wrote his old girlfriend to apologize. She wrote back telling me, "Thank you." She too had been trapped. She listed the same pattern, major debt, ruined credit, emotional and mental abuse. Good God, this is what you see on *Dateline*! But I survived.

True to narcissistic form, at the end he decided it was for my career that we finally record all the music we had written and performed for eight years. He had withheld recording all the new music we had created simply because he knew it was what I wanted most, all the while watching him record with others. Another cruel power game. Instead of saying no and walking away hurt. I said yes! This was my music, and nothing was going to stand in the way of finally getting it recorded. I pushed my broken heart to the side and spent a total of 12-14 weeks over a year-and-a-half after I moved to Seattle, giving my all to the music. I now have the final masters of four CDs of original music. This has been an important part of my healing.

As I write, it is 2016 with three very challenging years to reclaiming my life behind me. The first thing I did was get into counseling. Then, I found movement classes, Soul Motion, Nia and Free Form Dance to get me back in my body. Feeling my spirit alive inside as I move helps me listen to my inner voice as it rises up and reminds me of who I really am. I got a job, pierced my nose, changed my hair, went to a new church, and started singing a cappella with a group of sweet wise women. I went bankrupt, got a newer car, and started healing my credit. I have recovered from two major surgeries and get massage and energy work when I can. I returned to singing and speaking professionally. I invested in a coaching program that has helped me grow by reflecting my value.

All along the way I have journaled, prayed, meditated, cried, grieved, forgiven, laughed, and listened in the silence. Nature and her love is a best friend. Every year is better than the one before. I have a vision for my life now that I didn't have six months ago. An awareness came to me recently that it has taken losing everything for me to find myself. To love and accept myself completely. Goddess, what a way to get here!

But I truly have no regrets. He was the hardest and best teacher. I grew in ways I didn't know I could. I have my voice, my music and message. I am alive with a new life bursting to be created. I can protect and take care of myself. I will love again. My heart and sexuality are healing. He didn't take that away. I am much wiser now.

The world is full of so much to not trust, created by humans. Yet the world is full of so much to trust, created by Creation itself! That is my touchstone, my love and my life. I am thankful to be alive.

Hopeless, Helpless and Powerless

by Maureen Gilbert

In order to understand hope, you first need to spend some time in despair. You need to see all your best efforts and ideas, your solutions for how to change your life and improve things, fall away without success. Then what. When you've tried everything and nothing has worked, what do you do? What inner resources and philosophy of life can you turn to when your best thinking has failed you? It has often been said that where God closes one door She opens another. However, as a good friend of mine said, "In the meantime it's hell in the hallway." How do you find hope when it appears that your dreams have been shattered and your life is in ruins?

No one falls in love and gets married thinking that happily-ever-after would one day look like moving out of your house with two young kids to get away from your spouse with a substance abuse problem, having a business fail due to circumstances beyond your control, and ending up living in a small apartment barely making ends meet doing a job you can't stand. That's never the plan. Life and choices have a way of taking us down roads we'd never expect to go down.

If you rewind ten years you'd never guess that's where things were headed for me. I worked for a large international bank. I was living in Amsterdam with my husband. We were expecting our first child and after living as expats for several years and having successful corporate careers, we both decided to cash-out and buy a business in California. We bought a 20-room boutique hotel on the Mendocino Coast. We doubled the revenues, had a second child, and it felt like we were living the dream.

Then came the economic crash of 2008, a business partner who cheated us and ran off, and a client who trumped up a false lawsuit to extort money from us. We hobbled along for three years (yes, I am stubborn), during which time my husband chose clinical depression and substance abuse as his preferred means of dealing with the trauma that had entered our lives.

It was during these three years that I developed a very dysfunctional relationship with hope. In fact, I now joke that I was a "hopium addict." By that I mean that I regularly tried to fight against reality and the parts of my life that weren't working out; hoping that this time my imposed solutions would work, only to fall into despair when once again nothing had changed and I was still in a difficult situation.

It was during this time that I needed to get to know another quality: powerlessness. It took a lot of dysfunction and despair for me to finally give up my ironclad belief that I could control other people, places, and things, and that if I did I could master life. At that time my hope was misplaced because it was tied to certain outcomes. I was a victim of the delusion that I could wrest happiness or even satisfaction from life if only I managed well. Powerlessness puts us face-to-face with the humility that ultimately we aren't in charge of our lives and, while we may have influence, we can't control or guarantee outcomes regardless of how hard we try.

While this may sound downright depressing to many people and not very hopeful or inspiring, it must be coupled with the realization that powerless does not mean helpless. In other words I may not have control of the outcomes but there are some things over which I do have control:

1. My Story. I will have to call this an act of Grace because my ego definitely wanted to hold onto anger and resentment towards all the people who had wronged me. I was mad at my business partner; the woman who sued me; my husband; and, to be honest, even God. However, one night it hit me like a ton of bricks: I couldn't change what had happened, but if I gave those people and circumstances my serenity and joy, then they would have taken a lot more from me than just my money. I love the opening line of *Shataram* by Gregory David Roberts, "It took me a long time and most of the world to learn what I know about love and fate and the choices we make but the heart of it came to me in an instant while I was chained to a wall and being tortured. I realized that even in that shackled, bloody helplessness I was still free: free to hate the men that were torturing me or to forgive them. It doesn't sound like much… but when it's all you've got, that freedom is a universe of possibility. And the choice you make between hating and forgiving can become the story of your life."

2. My Behavior. It is so easy as Terry Real calls it to "offend from the

victim" position. In other words when someone or something does something to us that feels undeserved and wrong, it's easy to feel entitled to our own bad behavior. Who doesn't feel entitled to flip-off the person who cuts us off in traffic; break our diet "because we had a hard day;" yell at the kids because they "ignored me for the third time." However, doing that gives all our power to the other person or event. We are saying, essentially, "I am not free to choose who I want to be in this circumstance, I am merely a puppet and victim of what has happened to me. If I wanted to truly walk the talk of my spiritual practice I needed to be who I wanted to be and not allow circumstances to be an excuse for self righteous entitlement."

3. My Actions. The Yoga Sutra has the dual concepts of Abhyasa and Vairagya. They can be loosely translated into English as "never give up" and "always let go." In other words, never stop trying to move in the direction you want, but let go of attachment to results and outcomes. I might be powerless, but if I don't give up then I'm not helpless. The best analogy I have for this is gardening. If you want a plant to grow, there are certain things that are conducive to a healthy garden: planting a seed in good soil, watering it, making sure it gets adequate sun, pulling up weeds. However, ultimately you can't make a seed sprout. You can do everything right and still the seed might not sprout.

Back when I was a "hopium addict" my hope was tied to outcomes. I still hadn't let go. I hoped my husband would get into recovery, I hoped our business wouldn't fail, I hoped the lawsuit would be dismissed. Now I realize that hope is about planting the seed even if you have no guarantees that something will bloom. It's about accepting that although you might prefer certain results and outcomes, you will be okay even if the seed never sprouts. Most of all it's about a certain grit and faith in life that says you will plant the seed anyway, even if the outcome is uncertain because who you want to be in this world is someone who will plant the seed anyway.

My story does not have a Cinderella ending. My husband did not get help, the business did not survive, and the business partner and the lawsuit decimated my kids' college savings fund and our meager retirement accounts. However, if I had a choice between going what I went through and being the person I am today with the relationship I have with myself, my higher power, and with life, or to be who I was before all this happened, I would choose the former. Hope is now an inside job that knows that while life might not always be pretty or fun I will never be completely caught in the maelstrom of despair because I have practices, fellowship and a spiritual program that will sustain me even in the worst of times.

Sometimes you have to surrender to Win.

Why Can't It Be Me?

by Lisa Romeo

In the 1980s, three years after graduating from one of the country's top journalism schools, I was struggling to support myself as a freelance writer. Struggling was my choice since my father, who had grown wealthy manufacturing polyester, was willing to send me checks (or envelopes full of cash) each month. He was stubborn that way. But I was stubborn, too. I'd already turned down a low-paying but stable entry-level job at a tiny magazine for the unpredictable and precarious, but infinitely more exciting, world of freelance sports and feature writing.

Some months I secured enough writing assignments to pay all my bills and have some spare dollars, and told my father that business was booming. Other months, I skipped paying one bill or another. I never told my father about any of those months.

One afternoon in my New Jersey apartment, I was unloading a single grocery bag filled with boxes of pasta, a jar of peanut butter, and a six-pack of those highly salted instant noodle soups. My eyes fell once again on the mail stacked at the far end of the table I used for eating, writing, and late night crying. Tucked under the magazines I needed to read to plan future article pitches, and the classified section of that week's newspaper, and the bills, was a brochure for an upcoming conference held just across the Hudson River in New York City, the annual meeting of the American Society of Journalists and Authors (ASJA). At the conference, I knew I could learn from seasoned freelancers with decades of experience, hear about new ways of pitching editors, and get some practice in the one-on-one editor meetings.

The thought of attending was so alluring, so tempting and, finally, impossible. The fee would destroy my budget in any month. Shouldn't I stay home and spend those two days finding more assignments? Then again, was it possible that I'd learn enough at the conference to make a positive difference to my budget every month for months or years to come?

At the time, I was also reading a lot about how to be an independent contractor, and started to think of myself as the "owner" of my own little writing business. The advice writers, and sometimes my father, told me to consider marketing expenses, like the conference fee, a necessary investment in my future. Admitting to my father that I could use one of those envelopes of cash that month so I could attend the conference wasn't easy. But it also wasn't so hard. He understood and encouraged me to go, to attend every session, to pick as many brains as possible.

So I went. There, I made important contacts with editors who sent work my way for many years; discovered a few things I was doing wrong and so many things I could try doing differently, which made a big difference. Best of all, that conference gave me the confidence to expand into new territory I might have shied away from before. That conference, and eventually a handful of others, became must-do's on my annual calendar, and I worked steadily as a freelancer.

Then came kids. One kid who needed me more than usual. As motherhood expanded and, for a while, overtook my life, and my son's needs took over our budget, writing conferences again became luxury budget items, and slid off my calendar. Writing almost slid all the way off too, though I managed to churn out enough articles each year to stay in the good graces of a handful of editors. In the meantime, the internet exploded, and I found I could get my conference fix right at my dining room table from the advice available at my fingertips, connecting with other writers via blogs and later, social media. But I missed the in-person gatherings.

Eventually both of my kids needed me less, and I found myself at a new but familiar junction. I had just turned 50 when I had another afternoon like the one in the tiny studio apartment 25 years before. As usual, I was worried about money, since college loomed for my oldest child. Although by midlife I had been working steadily both in traditional jobs and as a freelance writer, and though I had plenty of confidence, maturity, and experience, I had to admit that in some ways, I was starting over. The freelance world had changed dramatically. So many of the print magazines, newspapers, and specialty publications I'd written for steadily had folded, and those that remained were tougher to crack. Writing for online venues was an entirely new challenge, demanding a different set of skills I wasn't sure I could master so many years after first learning the freelancing ropes.

One afternoon in my suburban New Jersey house, while cooking a batch of vegetable soup, my eyes kept drifting to my laptop screen. Blinking there was a notice of the approaching ASJA conference in Manhattan. It had been many years since my last conference, more than two decades since that first one. But attending was so tempting. I lived just across the river. I wanted to expand my career and keep up with the changing freelance landscape. I really had no excuse. Except that the marketing expense money would be better spent on one child's cello lessons. The other's college visits. Or groceries.

While the soup simmered, I procrastinated by clicking over to a blog post by a writer friend; she was reminding readers that the deadline for the first ever ASJA Education Foundation Conference Scholarship was that very afternoon. Wait. A way to attend the conference at no cost? Alluring. I thought about applying, but immediately dismissed the notion, certain the selectors were looking for someone either with fewer publishing credits, in worse financial circumstances, and/or with less gray hairs.

Then I remembered something I'd heard echoed by both novelist Tayari Jones and memoir author Meredith Hall, two writers I admired. They both encouraged writers of all ages, of all experience levels, to think big, to be audacious, to ignore their inner critics; to even be a bit reckless in seeking out and applying for opportunities. Boiled down, their advice was this: Every day, someone is awarded something for which he or she may not seem precisely qualified. The trick is to keep applying, because one day, why can't it be you?

Hope winked at me from the screen. The scholarship application was due in a few hours.

Why can't it be me?

I made a cup of tea, sat and typed. I spent the most time on the question about why I thought the conference would help me at this particular time in my writing career. I was honest about it all: my age, my on-and-off career (subject to kids and special needs advocacy), my newbie status at the online demands of modern freelancing.

I hit send.

A month or so later, I was picking up my badge at the conference registration desk when the ASJA president approached to congratulate me on receiving the scholarship, which covered my conference fees in full.

"I'm so grateful," I told her. "I almost didn't apply because I thought you'd want someone younger or greener."

Not really, she said, they just wanted someone for whom the scholarship would make a clear difference.

It made a difference.

As I'd done in my 20s, I met editors face-to-face and gathered useful intel about how to snag more assignments. I asked questions, listened, and absorbed all I could, in real time. I shared a meal, and ideas, with people I might not have sought out, but who had lessons to offer. On the train home, hope renewed, I made lists of possibilities.

That was more than five years ago. Since then, I've taken a lot more chances. I work every day at being a little more audacious, going after writing assignments I may not be one hundred percent right for. I write frequently for online venues.

Eventually, I began teaching writing online. One goal was to encourage others to keep seeking opportunities because one day, it could be them winning a contest, getting hired for an assignment, receiving an award, earning a scholarship.

About three years after she'd taken one of my classes, a writer in her late 20s emailed to say she was moving to Brooklyn, and could we have a cup of coffee in Manhattan? I asked if she'd be at the upcoming ASJA conference. Nope, she said, can't afford it. I sent her the link to the conference scholarship, and the prompt: Why not? Why can't it be you?

You know the rest. She received the scholarship. We shared lunch at the conference where, this time, I was one of those presenting information to help other writers.

Since then, I keep giving all writers, and all the teenagers in my house, and all people, period — young, old, less- and more-experienced — the same audacious, reckless advice. Apply. Try. Ask. Risk. Put yourself in the mix. Why can't it be you? I plan to follow that advice until I can no longer move my fingers across the keyboard.

Releasing The Kraken

by Janel Gradowski

Family relationships are like being on a cruise ship. When everybody is happy and enjoys being around each other, it's smooth sailing with sunny skies and umbrella-festooned cocktails by the pool. If the relationship isn't so great, it is like having a kraken leashed to the bow. You never know when a tentacle will grab hold of the rudder to steer your plans off-course or the entire, scary creature will leap out of the water and try to pull you under.

For many years, my coping strategy was to maintain a distant, superficial relationship with my parents. I have now realized that pretending that I am fine with the way they behave and treat others is akin to tossing food scraps over the side of my ship to keep the sea monster close. All that leads to is more stress and apprehension. I am the introverted daughter of narcissists. Our views of a life well-lived diverged when I was a teenager and have never drawn closer.

The out of sight/out of mind strategy worked quite well, until it was no longer possible to keep my distance thanks to a series of health crises that my parents weren't able to handle on their own. They needed my help. The protective mental shell that I had constructed throughout my adult life disintegrated more every time my father had an issue that required hospitalization. My world turned upside down as I spent countless hours at the hospital to keep track of his care while juggling my own life as a mother, wife, and writer. There was no time for me to also take care of myself, both mentally and physically. It was exhausting chaos.

In the summer of 2015, a month after the most recent health drama, I was still too tired and stressed to do anything with my husband or children. We had spent what was supposed to be our family vacation shuttling back and forth between our home, my parents' house, and the hospital instead. The career I had dreamed about doing since I was a child was falling apart. I was a bestselling author and my next book was due in a few months, but I couldn't write. My creativity was gone. The constant question in my mind was: how was I going to be "good" and help my parents yet not let their issues take over my own life? I needed to get over my fear of the kraken and learn how to make peace with it, but I had no idea how to accomplish that. I would need to sail into uncharted territory.

I started by attending caretaker support group meetings. The first few meetings were a relief; finding other people who understood what I was going through because they had been there, too. But then I began feeling burdened, instead of lighter, when I attended. It seemed as though I was absorbing the sadness and despair of the other people as they talked about their spouses no longer recognizing them or the last moments of a loved one's life. I stopped going to the meetings because I couldn't bear them anymore.

It was clear to me that I needed help as much as my parents did, but I wasn't sure where to turn. I wasn't a member of a church and had no spiritual practice of my own. In fact, at that point I hadn't yet realized that there was a difference between spirituality and religion. For multiple reasons I've had an aversion to organized religion since I was a teen. I was very distrustful of anything religious or woo-woo, my term for spiritual or New Age practices. Yet somehow I discovered the book *Soul Shifts* by Dr. Barbara DeAngelis. The description intrigued me, so I bought it. As I read about people giving off high or low, positive or negative, vibrations that others could feel, a lot of things suddenly made sense, like why the caretaker meetings became draining instead of helpful.

I was intrigued to learn that I could counteract the low vibrations that I was picking up from other people by raising my own vibrations so high that the negativity couldn't affect me. It sounded good on paper, but I was skeptical. When I found out I needed to accompany my father to a doctor's appointment where he would be getting some bad news, I decided to give it a try.

The night before the appointment I went to a reiki-share event for the first time. I wasn't sure energy healing would help, but I figured it couldn't hurt. It was a lovely experience. I only freaked out a little bit when I felt a hot stream of energy flowing through my arm at one point. Afterward a woman took me aside and gave me some advice on how to help my father cope with the news he would be receiving by my generating positive energy and directing it toward him. As my husband drove my father and me to the doctor's office, I concentrated on broadcasting peace and calm. I imagined those positive feelings as a mist radiating from me and filling the interior of the vehicle.

Did it work? Yes! My husband and I were both stunned at how calmly my father accepted the distressing prognosis. It certainly wasn't the reaction we had expected.

That experience was literally life-changing for me. I transmit positive or negative energy like a radio tower. I had the power to stop the downward energy spiral I tumbled into every time I had to draw close to the negativity I often felt from my family members or other people. While picking up on other people's emotions might be handy at a poker game, it isn't fun to soak up someone else's anger or resentment. I've learned to try to deflect or boomerang negative attitudes with a sort of force field generated from awareness. I see your negative emotions. I choose not to feel them too.

After feeling victimized by the actions and attitudes of others for so long, the ability to counteract the darkness was empowering. My bonds to the unwanted, for my part, family drama began to weaken. I realized that not only had I unconsciously taken on the emotions of others, I had also put the burden of dealing with the consequences of their choices on myself. Why? I'm honestly not sure. I have always avoided conflict. For most of my life I would rather quietly do unpleasant things instead of protesting or refusing, because I didn't want to rock the boat by making someone upset. Most of my long-standing inner turmoil has come from wanting family members to do the "right" things: treat each other with respect and kindness, stop ignoring medical issues until they became serious emergencies, to quit alienating themselves by saying rude or offensive things. I have discovered that when I lower my expectations and let go of my desire to be right, I'm far less disappointed and stressed out. Just as every person is unique, so is their perspective on how to best handle situations and deal with any consequences. I try my best to live and let live, but it isn't always easy when my life is being affected by another person's choices.

Recently a friend suggested using a mantra when I begin to feel overwhelmed: I am enough. It's a wonderful thought, but I distilled it into the true essence of what I had been feeling for a long time yet hadn't had the courage to say: Enough! I've had enough of trying to repair relationship bridges that I didn't burn. I've had enough of missing out on the things in life that really matter to me because I've been too busy trying to please everybody else. I've had enough of dragging around the kraken when I really want to just enjoy the cruise.

So how do I set myself free? I make priorities and fiercely protect them. I say no to things that I don't want to do, even if others are disappointed. Journaling helps untangle knots of thoughts by giving them someplace else to live, besides my mind. It's also a great way to vent when things aren't going well.

Making radical changes in life can get messy sometimes. Pages can be ripped out and thrown away or even burned as a very literal way to get rid of the bad juju that was poured out on the paper. Playing with my dog never fails to make me laugh. I meditate to help stay calm and focused. I shut my computer off as early as possible and read something enjoyable to gently wind down the day. I'm training myself to find happiness and serenity no matter what is happening around me. It's a good skill to have.

Maybe the most important thing of all is that I try not to worry so much, even though it's something that I have done excessively my entire life. One of my favorite quotes is from Gabrielle Bernstein: "Worry is a prayer for chaos." Experience has shown me that I can imagine twenty different scenarios, yet something completely different that I hadn't thought of will actually occur. So why waste my energy trying to predict the future? I still prepare by doing research and considering options, if necessary, but I try my best to refrain from unproductive worrying about outcomes that I often have little to no control over. There are so many other wonderful things to use that energy for, such as spending time with my kids, cooking a nourishing meal, or listening to an inspiring podcast.

I have accumulated a set of tools that I've used to break the chain and set the relationship kraken free. It is still swimming around nearby. Sometimes it breaks the surface, and I'm filled with familiar fear. Then I remind myself to take a deep breath. I've been through things like this before and survived. Now I have the knowledge and skills to navigate through rough water. I'll be okay.

My Hero Has Wings

by Ashley H

"Never say goodbye, because goodbye means forever."

That was one of the things that my grandmother was always famous for saying, though I never quite understood it growing up. When something exciting was going to happen, like a trip to an amusement park or a family party, "forever" felt like the length of time until whatever it was happened. All of my friendships made through the years when I was younger were supposed last "forever." When I got into the higher grades in school, when recess went away and things were no longer fun, it seemed like it was always "forever" until summer finally came back around and I was free for a few months. When I was a teenager and started dating, "forever" was how long any relationship I got into was supposed to last. So, how was I supposed to know how long "forever" really was? Forever seemed like a long time, but it always came. Did anyone ever know how long forever really was?

My grandmother was so much more than a grandmother to me. She was my legal guardian until I was considered a legal adult. But even more than that, she was my second mother. My mom always was and always will be the person who gave birth to me, but my grandmother raised me. She took me in, even when there was barely any room in her already small apartment. She worked twice as hard to make sure she could provide for me as well as herself and my youngest uncle who basically was more of a brother than an uncle.

There were so many times that my grandmother went without just to make sure I had everything I needed and she gave me every single thing she possibly could have. But the things that were most important that she gave me were things that couldn't be bought. She gave me her time, patience, and love. She was the one person who never gave up on me; not when I was a whiny six-year old with a cold, not when I was a prissy pre-teen thinking I knew everything, not even when I was a teenager battling depression and heartbreak, thinking that everyone hated me. She didn't give up on me when she was diagnosed with cancer and fighting for her life, when the cancer came back a second time and she had to fight even harder, when she received the terrifying news that she had a terminal illness and only months to live, not even when she started losing her memory rapidly due to the terminal illness. I was always "her girl."

I prayed every single day from when she was given only months to live until her last day alive that the test and scans were wrong, even though I knew they weren't; it became clearer with every passing hour that she was getting worse. On a cold night, in the beginning of March when I was eighteen years old and three months pregnant, my grandmother passed away. That is when I learned what "forever" really felt like. Forever wasn't a few days, weeks, months, or even years. Forever was just that: forever; until the end of time.

Things were never quite right after my grandmother left us. The family fell apart, we struggled harder than ever to make ends meet, bills went unpaid, and there was so much that a baby needed when they came into this world. By the end of each month we were counting pennies to survive. We let the phone constantly ring with calls from bills collectors and went to sleep each night wondering whether or not, when morning came, we'd have a simple luxury that so many people take for granted such as heat or electricity.

All public assistance programs turned us down, those of us who were unemployed, including myself, couldn't find work anywhere. It was a very dark time with almost no hope for the future and the little wiggling bundle of life that was growing inside of my body made me even more anxious because I had to wonder how we were going to make it with a newborn in the house when we were barely getting by ourselves.

Almost six months later, I gave birth to the most perfect baby boy that I have ever seen. I made it through the labor and delivery with minor struggles and he was healthy. He had the most beautiful blue eyes that I have ever seen and I wished so badly that my grandmother had gotten the chance to meet him. There was a lot of joy throughout the family, the kind of joy that only a new baby can bring. However, that joy was short lived. The reality of life set back in rather quickly. Things still weren't good financially, almost everyone was exhausted from helping me out with the baby, most people (including myself) were still grieving from the loss of my grandmother. It felt like, now more than ever, there was no hope for the future.

I found myself thinking about my grandmother a lot. I wondered what she would do if she were faced with a situation like this. Then I remembered: there were plenty of times that she had gone through things like this. There were a lot times when she didn't know how she was going to make it, but she always did. It didn't matter what it took, she always made it and I was just realizing that it wasn't ever herself that she made it through for; it was her children and then me. There were so many nights that she was exhausted from working two jobs, so many times she was sick and still worked 12 or more hours a day only to come home and help me with homework, do housework, put me to bed, and still get me on the school bus bright and early in the morning before doing it all again.I never saw her break down. I never saw her give up. She kept going. Her strength gave me a little bit of hope for the future. Enough hope to hang on for another day.

Things seemed to move extremely slow, but progress was made. I eventually started college (which is what I had always wanted to do), got a job, and found a more affordable home for my own little family. It was a long process, but I remembered who I was doing it for. It wasn't for me or about me anymore. It was for and about my little boy. My grandmother fought hard and kept pushing forward for me, it was time for me to fight as hard as I needed to and keep pushing forward for my son. To this day I still have hope for our futures, even when times are tough, because of my grandmother. Even though she isn't physically with me anymore, she has still managed to influence my life greatly. She gave my hope back after I had lost it, even though she was no longer here.

Tough times happen to everyone. Things happen that are out of our control. Throughout my life so far, I have witnessed a lot of these things happen and experienced them myself. I know some things are harder to deal with than others, particularly those events that remove a person from our lives forever, such as death. If you are in a tough situation, I think it is important to remember that you are not the only person who has gone through it, is going through it, or will go through it. It is also important to know that it is okay to feel down-and-out; it is okay if you temporarily lose hope. I think we all feel that way about something at some point in time. However, the most important thing I can tell any-one to remember is that you need to keep moving forward, regardless of what that means to you. You may feel sad, angry, upset, or hurt, but you still need to wake up every morning and keep going.

Believe it or not, heroes exist, and they are not the made up characters in comic books or movies. There are those obvious heroes like police, firefighters, EMTs, and so on, but we also have our own personal heroes. They can be a parent, relative, or even friend. We are sometimes so busy living life that we take simple things for granted like having someone to talk to, a shoulder to cry on, or a place to turn for guidance when you feel lost. Turn to your family and friends during your tough times of life. They are your heroes during these times. They will help you. I didn't believe in heroes myself, until I realized that I actually have had a hero watching over me whole life; and now my hero has wings.

Period of Recovery

by Bear Kosik

I began working on my sobriety around Halloween in 2002. Around that time, I pulled out a play I had been working on for almost twenty years. Called *Father's Day*, it arose from a poem I wrote after my father died suddenly at 52 years old. My father was a recovering alcoholic. In the fifteen or so years during which I had been drinking heavily, it never really crossed my mind to seek help as he did. I finally had done something when serious health issues arose. Doing something and being successful are two different things. The one requires hope and the other sees that hope fulfilled.

I finished the play around the time I finally stopped drinking in July 2003. It was the first bit of creative writing I had completed since my early twenties, since the poem that generated the play. Happy to have been productive even while struggling to put the plug in the jug, I started working on another play called *Mother Explains* that I had been keeping notes for. I had a stack of papers, notebooks, and Post-Its on which I had scribbled thoughts, ideas, and bits of dialogue over the years. It seemed like a good idea to connect with the person I was before I started drinking alcoholically, to the guy who dreamed of being a writer.

Over the next few years, I completed the play. By that time, I had changed jobs to something that was more challenging and paid less. But it was a job where I had never shown up drunk. That was what mattered most. When I chanced upon a notice in the newspaper that the Classic Theatre Guild was looking for works for their New Play Festival in 2008, I submitted *Mother Explains*. It was the first time I had ever submitted a play anywhere. That made it all the more wonderful when they said they wanted it for a staged reading.

Working with the actors and having an audience hear my work and laugh, forever altered my view of myself. I had not pursued being a writer earlier in life due to issues of low self-esteem and the vagaries of becoming successful in that profession. Now, with a secure job and five years of sobriety to testify to my abilities and strengths, I could accept putting my soul out in the world through writing and have people decide whether or not they understood it and appreciated it. Listening to the generally positive and absolutely helpful feedback from the audience, I became a writer, not just someone who writes.

The following year, I had a short play accepted for the 2009 festival. By then, my job and hobbies were fulfilling enough that I sat back and enjoyed the feeling of finally having accomplished what I had wanted since I was a teenager. I was in no hurry to push forward as a writer because I felt confident it was something I could do ten or fifteen years from then in retirement. I went back to just keeping notes and occasionally focusing on a project.

Then, beginning in early 2011, my world came crashing down. I broke two fingers on my right hand that ultimately left me somewhat disabled. I failed to get a promotion that had seemed tailor-made for me, the first and only time I have ever sought a promotion. That was okay, because I still had plenty of autonomy in my job and enjoyed what I was doing. However, the person who eventually took the position turned out to be controlling harridan. All my life, I had reported to people who had treated me as a collegial partner, not as an underling expected to do as he was told without providing input.

Meanwhile, people in my circles started dying, eight in all over a ten-month period. I was targeted for harassment due to my activities as a union president. In December 2012 I had to go on medical leave. The administrators of the college where I worked got what they wanted. I was terminated because they supposedly could not reasonably accommodate the disabling conditions created by my boss' vitriolic attacks and the harassment.

I learned that I could not get references or even acknowledgement of my employment at the college. That prevented me from finding employment in my field. I was overqualified for hourly jobs in stores and such. Managers point-blank said they would not hire me because I might get bored or find something better. What was not said, but was obvious from who was being hired, was my age was seen as a minus rather than the plus it should have been. I tried insurance sales twice. Despite succeeding in training, I could not establish any clients and wound up losing money on gas and incidental work supplies.

In June 2014, I took the advice of my spouse and my mother and decided I had been forced into early retirement. I was 53 years old, one year older than when my father died, with no hope of ever finding a consistent stream of income to replace what I had lost. Since I had always planned to turn to writing when I retired, that's what I did to fill my days. I started a nonfiction book on the state of democracy in the USA. I wrote essays. I cleaned up poems I had written three decades earlier. I started writing the book for a jukebox musical. I pulled together notes I had for a novel set in a post-apocalyptic future.

The last one turned out to be the first major work I completed as a full-time writer. I responded to a call for submissions posted by a publisher on LinkedIn. Within three weeks, I had a contract. Four weeks after that, I gave the manuscript to an adjunct English professor at the college from which I had been fired and paid her to check the manuscript for grammatical errors and typos. Three weeks more, the manuscript was in the publisher's inbox. Six weeks later, I was a published author.

I was seventeen when I sent a poem to a college review. It was accepted and I had hope. Thirty years later that hope was still there and now strengthened when my play was accepted for a staged reading. Six years on, hope took off with the contract for the novel. Since then, I have continued to be fortunate to have had a run of freshman luck in terms of placing my work. I saw my first essay, ten-minute play, one-act, short story, and flash fiction all accepted by journals and theaters.

While I consider myself successful in terms of being published and produced, I have earned very little in royalties. The income stream I lost three and a half years ago has not been replaced and is unlikely to be replaced. What marketing I have been doing has been wasted because my books have so few reviews, I can't afford to pay for more professional reviews, and nothing I have done to obtain more reviews from authors and readers has worked. I am still building an inventory of work to have more avenues for people to find me. Absent a miraculous breakout for one of my books, a renowned regional theater choosing one of my full length plays, or someone optioning one of my screenplays or television pilots, writing will never be profitable for me. I continue to write because it is spiritually and psychologically rewarding. I write because I discovered I am a writer. I write because I hope for that breakout.

I still stay away from booze. I evaluate who I am and who I want to be daily. It's not always easy. When I look at the news or listen to people talking about their views and their wishes, the dissatisfaction with life hangs there like fog over a river. The country has needed to go through the same sort of process of recovery as I have in the last fourteen years. It hasn't. Some people are not ready to admit we have a problem; others are not identifying the problem correctly. I don't see healing taking place. Instead, everyone is picking at the wounds and it's still messy. It is difficult to maintain any sense of a positive future.

On top of that, most of what has happened in my life in the last four years has been bad. It has been particularly so in 2016. Six people who have been important in my life have died since the end of January, a repeat of 2012. I destroyed my left knee in a fall in July. I see that was the result of a hazard that should have been taken care of, but I have been told I have no claim against the property owner. Any kind of settlement would have been an enormous help to my finances.

On the other hand, I have had three short plays produced off-off-Broadway and have released three books this year. Another novel came out around Thanksgiving from a Canadian publisher and another play opened then, too. I am working on several fun projects, including a television sitcom pilot.

As awful as it is to have things I have submitted rejected, I can reasonably hope that my work will be accepted for publication or production if I find the right venue. I do not have the false hope of someone playing the lottery where all is left to chance. I know I have some measure of talent that makes my writing worthy of being purchased. People from all walks of life and different backgrounds have told me how much they enjoy my work. That is a rock-solid foundation for continuing on this path regardless of the amount of compensation. My hope is grounded in the knowledge that I am a writer and not just someone who says he writes.

Praying on the Job

by Lisa Braxton

"I got the job," Alex announced as he let his keys drop onto the table by the front door. I wasn't sure how to react. Normally a job offer calls for some kind of celebration or at least an acknowledgement. But my husband didn't seem to be in the mood for either. The resignation in his voice was more pronounced than usual.

"How many hours will they give you?" I was willing my voice to sound upbeat.

He shrugged. "Don't know. They haven't posted the schedule yet. All I know is that I'll be working 11 in the evening until 6 in the morning." In his mid-50s, Alex had spent the majority of his career as a journalist, reporting for some of the nation's top newspapers, including The New York Times. He'd won an award for his reporting, rose to newsroom bureau chief, and became an adjunct instructor at the university where he earned his degree. He later left journalism to become associate director of public relations for a prominent research university. But after eight years there, he was looking for new challenges and took a position with a nonprofit anti-poverty organization. He was drawn to the organization's mission and the potential for additional responsibilities. I admired him for his willingness to take a pay cut for the opportunity to work directly with people who had limited means to advance economically. However, the job didn't work out. Within weeks of being hired, he was let go.

For the next six months, Alex doggedly pursued job openings in his field. We worked as a team. I helped him edit his resume and polish his cover letter. He beefed up his online presence. I helped select and post his headshot for the upgrade on a career-oriented social networking site. We role-played interviews well into the evenings after I'd come home from work. Companies began responding. Every so often, he'd come home ebullient, telling me that an interview was a "15" on a scale of "1" to "10." Sometimes he was called back for a second and third interview. We'd grow more elated at each of these stages, feeling that it was a sign that he would soon get a job offer. Cautiously optimistic, we'd get down on our knees before bedtime and pray that God would grant him the position. Yet, Alex didn't get any offers. He was told he was overqualified, or that he didn't have enough skills in an area that he, in fact, had plenty of experience in. Sometimes he was informed that the company was continuing to interview candidates, a euphemism for "we're not interested."

"I'm really sorry," he said, slumping into a kitchen chair. "You didn't sign up for this. It's not fair to you. I wouldn't blame you if you wanted me to go."

Alex's job loss had been a strain on our bank accounts and our relationship. We hadn't been married long — a month shy of two years — when he was let go by the nonprofit. Since then he'd only been able to contribute a fraction of what he normally put toward household expenses. Once his unemployment ran out, he was able to provide even less.

Now he'd be stocking shelves on the overnight shift at the supermarket down the street from our home. The pay wouldn't be much, but whatever he'd be able to bring home would help.

When we first married, we paid our monthly bills with our combined incomes and put a significant amount of money into savings. We talked about one day moving out of our small condo unit into a larger townhome or single-family home. I longed for more closet space and we both wanted to have additional room so that family members or friends could stay overnight comfortably. But after Alex became unemployed, we stopped talking about these goals. I was barely able to cover the bills on my paycheck. Adding to our problems was the condition of my car. I needed to replace the rusted-out 14-year-old vehicle, but couldn't chance pulling money from my account for a down payment in case we needed it for an emergency. Even if I decided to take the risk, I'd still have to deal with monthly payments, which I couldn't afford. Every few weeks when my car broke down, I had no choice but to patch it up, charging the repairs to my credit card and accumulating hundreds of dollars in debt. Alex never knew when he was going to get a call from me in a panic, stranded somewhere because my car wouldn't start.

I began having trouble sleeping, worrying that Alex might never get hired for a decent job again. I knew that when he suggested that I'd want him to leave, he wasn't serious. But I began to fear that one day he would give up on finding a job, give up on the marriage and walk away.

"You should come to prayer group," J.D. said. We were taking one of our regular lunchtime walks around the office park. I'd grown to cherish my co-worker's friendship. She was one of the few people I told when I went on my first date with Alex. After he proposed, she rode with me hours away from the community where we lived to a bridal shop in a neighboring state to help pick out my bridal gown, and was our greeter as guests arrived for the wedding ceremony.

The first time J.D invited me to the Friday morning group meeting was more than a year earlier. Initially I wasn't interested. I was a regular churchgoer and didn't think a group at work could offer me anything I wasn't already getting at Sunday morning services. Also, I didn't want to share something as personal as my worship life with individuals I didn't know that well. I was in a building with more than 300 people, most whom I didn't work with directly. However, because of the struggles Alex and I were facing, I began reconsidering J.D.'s invitation.

When she led the way into the conference room, I was relieved to see that the group was small. No more than seven or eight participants were seated around the table. Still, it felt awkward. I took my seat with people who I'd exchanged pleasantries with for years, but hadn't gotten to know.

The participants to the left and right of me extended their hands in my direction. It took me a moment to figure out that we were forming a prayer circle. During the 30 minutes that we had together, a co-worker played a familiar gospel tune on her iPhone. After a scripture reading, it was time for prayer requests. I thought about asking for prayer for Alex and me, but hesitated, too embarrassed to share our problems with the group.

When I got home that day, Alex's mood lifted when I told him about the prayer group meeting. "I'm glad you're getting involved with that," he said. "Prayer is important."

His words and J.D.'s prodding convinced me to go back the following week and share our story of struggle. In time I learned of the troubles facing my co-workers. One announced that her daughter had been recently diagnosed with mental illness. Another sought prayer for a parent's open-heart surgery. We prayed for employees who weren't part of the group, in particular a staff member whose cancer had spread to multiple organs and who was now on experimental drugs.

In time, I was assigned to be the worship leader. I'd read through Bible passages and devotionals to put together a meaningful message for the members of the group. It was rewarding to feel that I was playing a small part in their spiritual walk. I not only developed an appreciation for my co-workers, but gained deeper respect for my employer. Not all workplaces would allow staff to have time to worship.

Each week the group prayed that Alex would be hired for a position in his field, my ability to support him, and relief from the strain on our relationship. Even on the Fridays that I couldn't be there, they prayed for us.

Whenever Alex had job interviews scheduled he'd stop me on my way out the door to work. "Are you going to prayer meeting?" he'd ask. It was in those moments that I realized that the meetings were as important to him as they were to me.

One day, a member of the prayer group stopped me in the hall and asked how Alex and I were doing. I told her that he was still working the hourly job and hadn't gotten any offers in his profession.

"I'm praying for you," she said quietly to be discreet. "I think about you often."

Taking the advice of J.D. and opening my heart to my co-workers has not only provided spiritual support for Alex and me during our difficult time, but also helps me to feel less isolated at work. I have developed a connection with the members of the prayer group, like-minded co-workers who are caring and supportive.

As we face whatever is to come, Alex and I feel encouraged to not give up on our future.

How Hope Brought Me to the Other Side of Misery

by Clara Freeman

A pivotal time in my life that would alter how I viewed the world, and chart the course for the remainder of my life, came in January of 2000 when my marriage of twenty years fell apart. During the course of separating from my husband and finding a place to live, I would lose my nursing job of two decades, a dear friend and colleague, and my grown children would leave me an empty-nester. I was also still coping with the earlier losses of a younger brother and my dad and all the emotional baggage that unfolded and came rushing in to topple me and send me into a dark space of "woe is me."

Clarity didn't miraculously come in the morning after leaving my marriage. It took many months of wallowing in my own self-pity, prayer, and determination to get back to a place of hope and peace inside myself. Feeling helpless, hopeless, and alone in those terrible days, I had taken to my bed and consoled myself with candies, chips, and daytime soaps: my new bosom buddies. It was ironic that while I lay in slumber, dulled by *As the World Turns*, beyond my secluded walls, the world was truly alive and vibrant!

In the beginning of this unknown journey, I was angry and bitter and thought the world owed me something for being the good person I was. The noise of vibrant living outside my doors, the phone barely ringing anymore, and the soaps that became predictable monsters of fantasy, gave me pause and I realized for certain that every one of us is responsible for our own happiness. I had to decide if I wanted to survive where I was or thrive in the world as a productive member of society.

I had gone through a lot and it seemed it was more than one person should ever have to bear, because I was physically, mentally, and emotionally drained. I was also spiritually wanting, but I also knew that God doesn't give us more than we can bear and I had a choice to make.

It would be hard not to just give up and give in and live a listless and uncaring life, but somewhere inside myself I heard my mama's voice saying, "as much faith as a mustard seed." I was stronger than I knew and somewhere in the depths of my weariness, there was a glimmer of hope and faith. I would have to take baby steps, but one step at a time, headed in the right direction by doing work that I love, keeps me from succumbing to the ills of the world and leads me back from a dark despair to a bright light of optimistic *hope*.

I've always prided myself on being a realist, someone who knows that life never promised a rose garden, and that through hard work and determination, we can achieve the things in life that will provide for our comfort and well-being. I pretty much went through the first forty years of my life maintaining an optimistic view of life, even with the devastating deaths of my brother, sister, and parents. I remember talking to my primary doctor in 2006 about the sufferings I'd gone through over the years and she immediately prescribed a mild sedative. I am a nurse, so I knew that being prescribed anti-anxiety meds must mean that I was in a state of depression.

After about a week of taking the medication, however, I discarded them in my bathroom toilet. I didn't like feeling disconnected from reality or the physical wooziness of the medicine. I knew intuitively that I wasn't a good candidate for this treatment and this medicine wasn't going to become the cure-all for my particular struggle.

Instead, I returned to what I have been passionate about my whole life: writing. I had been a voracious reader and a closet writer since my early teens and found healing in the creative process. I recalled pulling myself out from a dark abyss after my brother's passing by writing away on my trusted Canon typewriter in the mid-eighties. A heartfelt one act play I wrote in his memory even caught the eye of a theater company in Louisville, who invited me to submit more of my work.

These days, I'm living an authentic lifestyle. I'm living a healthy and spiritually-aware lifestyle, and I'm using my gifts to help make life better for others. I'm determined that by sharing some of the wisdoms from my own life experiences, I can help another person live better, productive, and happier lives. I'm also a firm believer that God has you and me and "no weapon formed against us." I don't sit back and wait for something to happen; I have to plant the seeds of God's gifts to make my garden grow. Many of us look outside of our own truths for validation and hardly get to use the gifts we've been given to make a positive difference in the world.

I remember the feeling of hopelessness washing over me those months after my divorce. I'd had lost a brother, my dad, my marriage, my loved ones, my children, a dear friend, and my longtime job. I felt that no one cared about me and no knight in shining armor would be coming to rescue me. One day, while lying around watching soap operas and eating sweets, my ears heard the most joyful noises coming from outside my window. It was the noise of little children playing, horns beeping, truck rumbling down the street, and adult voices laughing in shared conversation.

I believe those sounds of life's vibrancy was God giving me hope in the choices I make. I could continue to lay around feeling sorry for myself, or I could chose to live and laugh and become better; for myself, for my loved ones, and for others out there needing to hear my story of how I came up from a place of hopelessness to hope.

I tell people that when facing setbacks and challenges in life, continue to move forward and focus on helping make someone else's life better. By forgetting about yourself and reaching out to help someone else, your blessings will always flow from the favor of the most high. It doesn't matter whether big or small, just reach out to offer your services and, sooner rather than later, you will find favor of positive shifts in your direction.

The Summer I Learned About True Friendships

by Darrell Gilkes

I thought I had been a good employee, and had worked my job faithfully for five years. I took care of mentally and physically disabled people for a municipal body. The job was something I felt I was passionate about.

I myself was physically disabled with Cerebral Palsy from birth, and was an aspiring teacher hoping to inspire special needs children to reach their potential. But by mid-2016, my job had become a sort of a nightmare.

There wasn't any singular reason why. Perhaps it was the fact that one of my bosses told my coworker that I wasn't to be trusted with certain participants due to my disability. Despite me explaining the situation to my other boss, she merely brushed it off as a "It's a he-said, she-said story and I can't prove anything" situation. Then again, it could've also been the fact that despite working hard for four years to get a promotion as a 23-year old, my boss kept awarding the job to high school kids instead of me. Or, perhaps it was the fact that everywhere I went, I was smothered by ex-close female friends who were slowly becoming ignorant to my existence, mostly due to the fact they had a boyfriend and didn't need me anymore. Regardless, it was August 12, 2016 when they came for me.

I remember crying so fiercely when they took me into the room. They started saying I was depressed and unfit for work, and I had been acting out. One of my coworkers must've told them something. The truth was, I had been depressed. Everywhere I looked at that job, I felt inferior.

I looked to my bosses, who ignored when I had been unjustly treated. I looked to my coworkers, who were given promotions over me and treated me like a social outcast. I looked inside myself, and realized how much of a mess I was. There was no way I could've ever succeeded at my job with that much baggage going on day-in and day-out.

After the meeting, one of my bosses drove me home, and I went into the house. I'll never forget the look on my mother's face as I explained the situation to her. I kept saying "I hope you're not mad at me." Because in the back of my head I consistently thought this was all my fault. I thought that all the bad things that had happened to me and all of these aforementioned injustices were things which I had somehow caused.

But the fact was, they weren't. And I needed to realize that.

No more than a few minutes after talking to my mom, I remember a message popped up on my phone saying "Anyone down for sushi?" on a group message. It was a good friend whom I had known from high school named Kelsey Fisher. I was so torn apart, and I didn't want to be alone, so I told everyone in the group about what had happened. No later than an hour after I sent that message, and a mere two hours from getting kicked out of my job, Kelsey had picked me up and we were on our way to sushi. I talked out the situation with her, and explained how unfair the whole thing felt to me. At the end of my venting, I'll never forget what Kelsey said to me:

"Well, thank goodness you don't work for them anymore. That's an awful situation to be in, and you don't deserve to be treated like that!"

That was the moment I realized it wasn't my fault; it was their fault. Kelsey was right: I didn't deserve to be treated like that. I deserved better than that. Looking back, that was the first step of climbing out of my depression. I had to stop blaming myself for the bad things that had happened to me.

It's strange how one sentence from an individual in a singular moment can make all the difference in your life! So I went home that day, really thinking about that idea. I found relief in it and I realized depression isn't something you do to yourself necessarily, it's something that can be caused by just having a terrible world around you.

Despite handing-in all the papers to my work from my doctor, saying that I was mentally fine to go back to work, my workplace never tried to contact me for the remainder of the summer. I found it insulting but at the same time relieving, because I knew that I wouldn't have to deal with those same people who treated me like garbage.

To make matters worse, I found out that my work had launched a formal investigation into why I was depressed. They spoke to the girls who had started to ignore me, in particular one whom I was interested in romantically but who rejected me. Under orders, she had been told that because of this she could no longer communicate with me in an attempt to "let me heal."

That distressed me a lot, because now they were also affecting my personal life and removing people who were close to me. At the end of it all, I was pretty much left with no friends from my old work. There was only one person who ever asked how I was feeling or doing throughout those weeks from my job. Shows just how valued I was by the people there. So with my old friends gone, and being pretty much blacklisted by my job, I was at an all-time low.

But instead of looking pessimistically at the whole situation. I forced myself to think positively about the whole situation. Yes, my friends are gone, but clearly they weren't the type to stick around. Yes, my job is gone, yet clearly they treated me horribly. However, despite many negatives to take out of the situation, there was also one great positive: I had freedom. I had three weeks to do whatever I wanted, whenever I wanted. There were no rules to what I could or couldn't do. I found excitement in that fact.

So I began planning a new path forward.

One special friend that had helped me do that was Eve Grosso. Eve and I had always been good friends throughout high school and university. Heck, I even took the girl to my high school prom and we won Prom King/Queen! But I remember after a few days after I had sent out that group text, she texted me and asked how I was doing. So I explained to her that I was doing fine, but that my life naturally was really bumpy right now due to what had happened.

What really surprised me was her next text, saying "I'm in town Friday, do you want to hang out then?" So I said yes, naturally feeling alone. Normally, Eve was the type of social butterfly who had dozens of friends to hang out with. The fact that she actively took time out of her life to drive over to my house and talk to me, meant the world to me. She and I went on a walk, where I discussed what was going on in my life. And she listened. Then she took me to McDonalds and got ice cream.

The fact that someone would take time out of their schedule to listen and cheer me up did something better than simply make me feel happy.

It made me feel valued.

To make someone feel valued is one of the greatest gifts you can give. Because with depression, self-worth becomes absolutely invisible. The events that had happened at my job made me feel like I didn't deserve equal respect, a promotion, or a decent amount of attention. All of these things made me devalue my self-worth. But because Eve had taken time out of her day, she had made me feel that I *did* deserve attention, that I was someone worthy of not only fixing but also being happy. That made me feel valued. Because of that, my self-worth and confidence had been restored, and I could start moving forward with my life again. I could have hope again.

Starting fresh again with self-worth, I gave myself the chance to re-evaluate my friendships. I set high standards for myself and the type of people I wanted as friends. I realized that those girls I was close with at my job were not the people I thought they were. The fact that neither one had even made an attempt to contact me, even after the job was over at the end of August, shows a lot about their lack of character. They're the type that smash people up and walk away from a situation without even thinking twice.

Moving forward, I had a new policy for the type of friends I wanted. I stopped putting in all the effort and let people come to me, because friendships ultimately are defined by how much effort you put into them. I abandoned the people who had abandoned me. Once I had removed those people, I was able to focus on the ones who really did care about me with much more value. People like Kelsey and Eve. You'd be surprised how much your self-esteem can go up when you stop wasting your time on people who won't give you theirs!

It was these new ideas and values that I used to rebuild myself and move on with my life. By the end of September I felt like I had beaten my depression. Do I still have moments where I look back and feel bad about what happened? Of course, but then I also remember how many bad things happened to me in my life when I did work that job. I can successfully say that I am a much better and happier person after leaving it all in the past. Sometimes, depression can be caused due to chemical imbalances. But in my case, it was just being surrounded in a toxic job, with toxic people, who didn't care much for me at the end of the day.

So if you're ever going through depression, be sure to ask yourself if it's really your fault. Are you to blame for the things going on around you? Chances are, you're probably not. Knowing that fact, you can fight back against it. Remove the people from your life you don't need anymore and invest more in the people whp do. Because those people are ultimately going to be the ones who will give you hope to keep going.

From Fear to Survival

by Diana Raab, Ph.D.

There was a while there when I lost hope that I would ever survive cancer, but my transformational story goes from fear... to surviving... to thriving. After my breast-cancer diagnosis in 2001 fear infiltrated my life, but with certain healing modalities hope returned, and I am now living in a very vibrant and productive manner.

"You will never look at life in the same way," a breast-cancer survivor told me just days after my mastectomy and reconstruction in 2001 at the age of 47. Her comment resonated with my belief that I could survive whatever life tossed in my direction. My transformation occurred in the realms of physical, spiritual, and emotional well-being.

Today, from a purely physical standpoint, I realize and accept that my body will never look and feel the same. My daily glances in the mirror continue to be a continual reminder of my journey. There's no escaping the truth. I can hide under my clothing, my covers, or in my closet, but underneath I must accept my new physical landscape. My bedroom has a full-length mirror, so unless I shut my eyes while getting dressed, I am reminded of my deformities. People say that scars give us character, and each day I diligently work to convince myself of this. I realize that the scars don't really matter when I remind myself that I have survived.

The phone call came in the spring of 2001.

"Hello, this is Mel Silverstein." Intuitively, I sensed that my doctor was phoning with bad news. I felt like ducking underneath my desk the way I did in elementary school in New York in the 1960s during nuclear-warfare drills. I wondered if anyone ever hid under a desk to protect themselves from getting a cancer diagnosis.

Part of me wanted to hang up the phone and let someone else do the listening, yet a voice in the corner of my mind whispered that I had to hear what my physician had to say. I took a deep breath.

"Well, Diana, there's good news and there's bad news. Is your husband with you?"

Within seconds, I completely lost my sense of focus and concentration.

"Yes. We're both here. We'll put you on speakerphone."

Dr. Silverstein said, "I'm calling to give you the biopsy results that just came in. As I said, there's good news and bad news. The biopsy did show DCIS; quite diffuse around the breast."

Suddenly, I felt myself slip out of the moment, far away into some other state of consciousness. Dr. Silverstein's voice sounded garbled among my inner mutterings. Denial overpowered me, and all of life's fears began to surface and whistle true.

He continued, "DCIS, or ductal carcinoma in situ, means that small cancer cells have begun to settle and grow in your mammary ducts. As far as I know, there is only some slight micro-invasion, but how extensive that really is, I won't know until more surgery is done."

Only fragments of his entire conversation were audible to me. When he uttered the word surgery, he lost me again. Surgery was my worst nightmare. As a registered nurse, I knew and understood everything that could go wrong. Plus, wasn't eight months of bed rest, one miscarriage, three cesareans, and knee surgery enough? I thought, how could one person endure more than that? Why me? The entire situation seemed surreal. Would there ever be peace in my life? I wanted to curl up and call it quits.

The phone conversation became a blur of dialogue echoing through my mind. I tried to deny everything the doctor was saying about my 47-year-old body, and for a split second, I wondered if Dr. Silverstein had gotten his patients mixed up. I desperately wanted that to be the case.

My eyes scanned my outdoor landscape, as if the swaying bamboo tree outside my office would offer some solace or explanation. I looked beyond to the blue sky sprinkled with clouds as the sun began setting upon the horizon. I had never prayed, but I looked up into the heavens and pleaded with my deceased father to make sure everything would be all right. He'd survived the Nazi Holocaust, and I hoped he'd help me survive this internal holocaust as well.

My eyes rolled toward the phone and then back into the eyes of my husband, and then toward the black-and-white school photos of our three children hanging on the wall. The innocence and love in their eyes caused me to tear up. I just couldn't focus on my doctor's words, as all I kept thinking was, "This must be a mistake, but I have to survive." We hung up, and my husband drew me close, holding me as tight as he did the day my father had died. I melted into him. As he had protected me so many times before, he promised to take care of me no matter what. I melted in his strong arms. For about five minutes, silence reverberated in the room, until he blurted out, "Fuck!" We looked at each other and collided foreheads as if that act would make the news sink in, or simply make it go away.

"You will survive and you will thrive. I know it," he whispered in my ear.

I wanted to die. That had to be a better alternative than mutilating the part of me that had nursed and nurtured all three of my children; the part of me symbolizing femininity, the part men were so taken with when they looked at women. For the first time in my life, I felt an overwhelming sense of helplessness. I would never have considered taking my life, but I saw a glimpse of what it might be like to be on the cusp of that thought.

In the end, I obviously survived the surgery and the emotional roller coaster that followed. I once read that some women become so jarred by the physical changes after breast cancer that many consider having an affair to reaffirm their femininity. But in my case, because of my passion for the healing power of words and teaching others to journal, I submerged myself in that task and decided to practice what I preached: writing for healing.

As my cancer journey continued, I became more sensitive to the comments of others during the discussion of breasts, artificial or otherwise. Also, on a spiritual level, the small things in life didn't seem to matter much anymore. It's not that I didn't get upset about the house being untidy or the dog prints on our car seats, but I came to realize what's truly important in life. For me it was my family, friends, and writing. That's where I decided to focus my energy. That's what helped me go on.

To help nourish my will to survive, I immersed myself in situations that made me feel good about myself, and surrounded myself with people with positive outlooks and good energy. I suppose this is what intuitively happens when you come face-to-face with your own mortality: you choose not to allow individuals into your life who drain you of the vital energy that will contribute to your own healing. It felt like my spirit's natural defense mechanism kicking in.

As a former nurse and caregiver, I had often been the person people ran to for assistance or emotional support. But although helping others still gives me a great deal of pleasure, I now ration the amount of time I devote to helping others. Before my surgery, I don't believe I worried too much about myself, but now I make a point of doing so.

In terms of my productivity, I've always been driven to get a lot done, but now there seems to be an added sense of urgency. Doctors say that my prognosis is extremely good, and that I will probably live to a ripe old age and die of something other than breast cancer. I'm glad to hear this because there's so much I want to accomplish. Since my cancer diagnosis, there seems to be a hidden clock ticking in my ear. I've always juggled working on a few books or projects at one a time, but these days I want to do even more. When you're diagnosed with something like cancer, the possibility of recurrence is always in the back of your mind, as much as you try to convince yourself otherwise.

I'll never forget what my oncologist told me just after my diagnosis: "If this condition or experience does not rivet your focus on life, then you've missed the point." As time goes on, I agree more and more with this sentiment. I realize how his words instilled in me a great deal of hope, even though after my diagnosis I did feel a huge sense of hopelessness.

My passion for writing helped me through this ordeal, and that's exactly what I recommend for others navigating similar or difficult journeys. Find a passion — something that makes your heart sing — and engulf yourself in it!

When Life Hands You Lemons

by Nancy Lynn White

"I'm sorry, but we're going to have to lay you off. Ms. Smith is waiting for you in Human Resources. She'll go over your separation packet
with you. You have the rest of the day to clean out your office. Someone
from Security will bring boxes, supervise the packing of your office, and
escort you out. Acme, Inc. and I wish you the very best of luck in whatever endeavor you choose in the future. I want to thank you for your
service." A hand is extended toward you expecting a parting acknowledgement.

How many of you have been on the receiving end of a rehearsed company speech such as the one above? A speech strategically designed to
strip the speaker of humanity while inflicting shock and emotional pain
on the unsuspecting recipient.

In the spring of 1988, a large corporation acquired my employer. As
things go after a big takeover, the following months revealed major
changes. Even so, I didn't see it coming. One Friday afternoon, at 5:30
p.m., my boss came into my office and plopped down in a chair across
from my desk with a deep sigh. I asked her what was wrong.

"Well, you know they've been talking about revamping our department since the takeover. Some decisions have been made."

"Really! What are they?" I relished the excitement of a new challenge.
She began at the top of our department organization chart, and one
by one explained the opportunities that lay ahead for my department
coworkers. She stopped at my position.

"Okay, great so far, what about me?" I asked in anticipation. "What's
new and interesting for me?"

"I'm sorry, but we're laying you off." Her shoulders dropped a little as
if relieved.

Why did she share all the wonderful opportunities ahead for others
just to tell me it ends today for me? After all those happy years, that was

it? I loved that company. It was in my blood. I spoke their language. I didn't know how to speak any other language. I planned on retiring from Acme, Inc. All of my performance reviews had been outstanding. My pay increases had been eight to ten percent a year. I was a stellar employee. Why? How could this happen to me?

The hardest part was not knowing why. What could I have done differently? How can I keep this from happening to me again? I drove myself crazy with unanswered questions. Running them through my head repeatedly, second-guessing everything I ever thought about myself. Was I really a capable person? Would I make a worthy job candidate? Every question I asked myself, my brain screamed "No!" I couldn't sell myself in a job interview. I didn't like myself. I had no value. I gave Acme, Inc. my best, only to meet rejection.

I cried constantly, seldom got out of bed and soon found myself paralyzed with depression. My husband assured me it was their loss, but I didn't believe him. This self-deprecating behavior went on for months. Thank God I had one very wise girlfriend. She checked in on me every once in a while, as I wallowed in my pit of despair. Then about a year into this obnoxious behavior she called one day and wanted company to go see a Brad Pitt movie. I declined.

"Exactly when was it that you gave Acme, Inc. power over your life?" She asked.

"What?" I asked totally missing her point.

"You're a great friend and I respect you, but it's time to snap out of whatever this is you're going through. I draw the line when my Brad Pitt buddy won't go to the movies with me. Excuse me for saying this, but take control of your life. Enough already. You've had a rotten break. We all agree. Get over it. Get a plan. And let's go to the movies."

She and Brad Pitt were absolutely right. When did I give that ungrateful company control over my heart and soul? Why am I taking a layoff personally? It's business! They do it all the time. You don't see laid off guys roaming their houses in robes and mumbling to themselves. Don't take it personal! Acme, Inc. was a business, not my life. The epiphany hit me smack in the forehead. My priorities needed serious reconsideration. My happiness is not dependent upon my place of employment.

What was I hoping to accomplish by hanging around my house whining when I can slip into some jeans and sneakers and go drool over Brad Pitt? In fact, the pre-show provided an excellent opportunity to badmouth my previous employer over popcorn and Diet Coke and seek advice from a valued friend at the same time. My girlfriend had no idea that she had lit the fuse on a stick of dynamite.

Time to get out and buy a new suit because Momma's going to land herself a much better job than the one she had before.

Yeah, I'd had a rotten break, but that rotten break's separation packet included job search assistance. I made an appointment. They paid for everything. Professional resume, interview training, and job search training. Thank you, previous employer.

Those nagging questions in my head were going to drive me crazy, so I had to get rid of them. The separation packet covered counseling to get back on my feet again if I needed it. My therapist introduced me to my long-lost sense of worth, but how was I going to keep this from happening to me again? I decided to get my college degree. I'm not saying that I'm immune to being laid off in the future because I have a college education, but my parachute has fewer holes in it.

I began college that fall full-time working on a B.A. in English. I was thirty-eight years old and had never been to college before. I thought getting laid off was tough, but compared to attending college full-time while working, it was a cake walk. It was about this time during a phone conversation with my sainted grandmother, that she gave me this wise advice. "Hard times will always come, but the smart ones learn from it and grow." I don't know why grandmas are always right, but they are. Thank you, Grandma.

I was amazed how many interviewers were impressed by the fact that I was going to college full-time. They tried to entice me to work for them by mentioning their tuition reimbursement program. Now companies vetted me. I landed a job with a newspaper paying $30,000 more than what I made before and they paid my tuition. Now, I was going to school full-time for free, working full-time, and taking care of my family. It was a circus, but an organized circus. My ego soared with the eagles. Thank you, family.

The newspaper employed me until I graduated and found a higher paying job with a manufacturing company. I don't put my heart into my job anymore because my heart is my power. I put my heart into my family, and I put my skills to work at my job. I cringe when I hear people say "I love my job." They go to work early, skip lunch and go home late like I used to do with a smile on their faces thinking they've done the best they can for that day. I feel sorry for them. I'm employed, but I work for me.

You're gone in the morning before your children are out of bed and home at night after they've gone to sleep. You've seen your spouse long enough to find out if the bills are paid and who's going to take the dry cleaning in on the weekend. You're too tired for little else because you put your heart into your job today. The sad part is in the grand scheme of things no one at work cares. Your boss isn't there counting the hours you put in, but your husband, wife, or kids are. You have to stop to ask yourself if its worth it? Am I truly appreciated for doing this day after day?

Take control of your life. It's your life. Take a spoonful of reality, swallow hard and sleep on it. The very next morning get to work on a plan and never look back.

Throw your bathrobe away. Spend time with the people who love you. Travel. The world is your oyster. Adopt a rescued pet. Do something you didn't have time to do when you had your rose-colored glasses on. Go to the park with your children, have a family picnic and bring your bikes along.

Cook pork chops in a rosemary reduction sauce, with grilled portabellas sautéed in wine, and for dessert, bread pudding with a warm whiskey sauce. Your family will be thrilled to spend time with you over the dinner table. Revive the art of family conversation. Beats Chinese takeout alone at work while you slave over your computer keyboard until eight or nine o'clock, then go home exhausted. You call that living?

Nothing ever "happens" to you. You're handed opportunities. Grow from them. Turn those lemons into lemonade to be served to your loved ones at dinner. And if an employer in the future gives you a devastating layoff speech, don't give them the satisfaction of looking disappointed. No matter what you do from that moment on, the fact that you're now unemployed by that company won't change. Smile, shake their extended hand vigorously and thank them. It'll make them nervous.

P.S. Acme, Inc. went out of business five years after they laid me off. I can't thank them enough for giving me the biggest break of my life.

Hidden Solace

by Elizabeth Philip

Come those first warmer days of late winter, I search for green shoots
spearing through the thawing ground. Spotting them, I dart into the
house to find my husband. "Michael, have you seen the daffodils?"
"No," he says, "are they here?" He's teasing me to prolong my excitement, and I appreciate his humor. Michael knows that the flowers are
more than harbingers of spring.

He accompanies me outside and stands close, caressing my shoulder
while his gaze follows my outstretched hand. I point to the clusters of
stems trickling down the hillside of our home. "Look here," I say, "and
over there." We delight in their abundance, the slow profusion from
year-to-year. Recalling the planting of 250 bulbs in rock-laden terrain
nearly ten years ago, we laugh at memories of broken trowels and blis-
tered hands. My labor arose from a need to understand my past, and
his labor reflected a need to understand me. Although I've never been
able to fully express the daffodils' significance in my life, my family
knows they're a symbol of something good and something comforting
amidst memories that are neither. Soon the flowers will bloom, and I'll
pay a daily visit, knowing they will perish in the heat of late spring, just
as suddenly as they arrived.

Long before I was old enough to read Wordsworth's poetry, the healing power of daffodils became evident with each trip to the creek. To
this day, the emergence of these golden flowers each spring instantly
transports me back forty years to a tranquil patch of land near my childhood home in Michigan. It was there I'd sit on a hollowed log to savor
the jonquils, an array of gold scattered across the meadow, coming to
life after the morning sun kissed the dew from their petals. Freed from
that burden, the flowers lifted their drowsy heads from the ground and
danced in the breeze blowing off Lake Michigan. I danced alongside
these messengers of spring, celebrating my escape from a recent winter's

fury of repeated bruises, stinging words, and unanswered pleas for help. This tranquil garden granted me hours of solitude and safety away from my home until dusk brought forth a chill that I could not ignore. As the daffodils toppled to the ground from the unwelcome dampness, I trudged home to accept my burden.

During the weekends and after school each day, my visits to this refuge allowed me to cast-off the shame of my mother's mental illness, my parents' volatile relationship, and the abuse I suffered after their fallouts. The sounds of nature muted the memories of my parents' hostile voices, the smacking of flesh on flesh, the scuffling of feet, and my mother's choked pleas that I call the police to save her, and his voice, in turn, demanding the same. But, most importantly, the daffodils — my confidants — cast no judgment upon me when I failed to dial the phone for either one of them. After all, how can an eight-year-old save someone else when she's busy saving herself?

If I set out for the creek early enough the next morning, my mother's displaced anger would find a different target, perhaps some kitchen glasses or a nearby vase. A sense of calm soothed my hopelessness when noting that the daffodils had endured the lingering effects of a late cold snap, an unexpected snow flurry, or even a layer of sleet. Despite such assaults, the flowers remained erect, like soldiers prepared for battle.

How I wished to be that strong. The daffodils' resolution was proof that life was worth fighting for and convinced me that no matter how unbearable my home life remained, determination could triumph over obstacles. Yet still, I longed to pluck the flowers from the ground to protect them from the harsh elements. But despite their discomfort, I knew they'd quickly perish if removed from their environment. So I left the daffodils to fend for themselves, praying each night that they'd survive another day; perhaps, the same prayer of the bystanders who chose to ignore the daily abuses taking place within the confines of my childhood home. It wasn't long before I realized that I'd have to save myself, and the inaction of others led to my self-reliance: a trait I shared with my beloved flowers.

Nature neither made promises, nor broke them; a comfort to a girl who felt safer outside her home than within. Unlike most children, I held no fear of the unknown since the known was surely worse. Wandering from home, I first stumbled upon the creek after journeying down a dirt pathway, cutting through an apple orchard, ambling past a dilapidated tree fort, and burrowing through some tall field grass. There, I heard the incantation of the creek as the bed filled with the melted snow of winter, carrying with it fall's deposits of leaves and limbs. The water was shallow in places, allowing me to skip from rock-to-rock and explore, even at the cost of muddied shoes. Grabbing a floating twig to pry loose a jam of debris, I delighted in the rush of water that had once been a mere trickle over the boulders. Time and again, I redirected the flow of the creek with a twig and a mere flick of my wrist. So powerful was I, deciding which barriers to leave in place and which to let go. It was here at the creek that I felt capable of setting the course of events to follow.

For many years, from the first thaw to the first frost, the creek and the daffodil field became my haven, my mentor. Forced to look inward, my special niche gave me time to reflect. To plan my survival. To plan my future. Here, I was no longer under the scrutiny of teachers, principals, or social workers, and avoided the questions that I dare not answer: "Where'd you get that cut on your lip?" and "Is someone hurting you?" At the creek, I was invisible in plain sight. Not even my family could find me and, in the absence of distractions, I was entranced by the subtleties of nature that most would fail to recognize: the patter of an acorn as it tumbled from leaf to leaf, the scuttling of a covey of quail in search of grubs in the field, the eerie stillness of a red-tailed hawk perched atop a fencepost awaiting the unsuspecting field mouse, and a glint of turquoise as a dragonfly hovered over the water before the hungry starling swooped down for a lively chase. The creek was a myriad of sights, smells, and sounds: graces that would take me years to appreciate.

In Michigan, the seasons were distinct, and I reveled in their gifts. Springtime brought the blooming of the daffodils, and I often wondered who had planted them. I envisioned a pioneer woman on her hands and knees for days, digging holes for the hardy flowers and patting them into place after tucking them safely into the ground. Had she wondered who would care for the magnificent flowers in her absence? Maybe she believed as I believed that anything that dared bloom with the lingering threat of a late-season snowstorm needn't warrant a hint of concern; the daffodils proved their durability with their emergence each year, teaching me yet another lesson: hardship begets fortitude. Solace at the creek continued long after the daffodils withered in the summer heat, and the rhythmic hum of cicadas often lulled me into an afternoon nap after searching the dry creek bed for treasures, like arrowheads, a shiny pop top, a feather from a blue jay, the shell of a crayfish, and a worn dog tag. I sat on smooth boulders and bathed in the sun sprinkling through the canopy of large oaks. The longer days were not only a gift to the local farmers but also a blessing to me, awarding me more time away from home. The chittering of a squirrel and the coo of a mourning dove quelled my vigilance and fear; all sounds natural and expected, unlike the cacophony between the walls of my home that served no purpose but to feed my fight-or-flight instinct.

Fall offered golden and russet foliage, the plucking of Red Delicious apples on my journey to the daffodil field, and occasional rainfall that sated the parched creek bed. The moist soil alongside the creek, along with the help of a broken tree limb, became a slate on which to list my hopes. I crouched and sketched words — "love," "dreams," and "family" — only to have them washed away with the next downpour. Then winter arrived, a time of hibernation for the creek and me. And I'd reluctantly tread home to await the call of spring.

Looking back, I'm not sure how I managed to endure those violent winter months. Yet, despite the prolonged, bitter season, I somehow reemerged hardier each spring, just like my daffodils.

Refuge, mentor, magic, all became internal, and the place became part of me. The daffodils remain vivid in my mind even though I haven't returned since I left Michigan in 1990. It's doubtful I'll journey back to the place that became my savior amidst a life of turmoil. Perhaps my decision is out of fear that the creek is no longer as I remember, or out of worry that the daffodil field has been plowed under. The need to preserve the only pleasures from my childhood outweighs the need to witness an unwelcome truth. Instead, I recreated my own field of daffodils, allowing me to reconnect with that little girl standing creekside, praying for a life so different than her own.

"Aren't the daffodils magnificent?" I ask, and I turn to Michael and smile.

He looks into my eyes with such understanding and tenderness that he need not say a word. Our hands interlock, and we journey up the hillside. The daffodils will soon bow their heads and sleep, knowing we're all safe for the night.

Against the Odds

by Jacqueline Seewald

I never thought I'd get married right out of college. But at twenty-one years of age, I met the man I would marry. I met my husband while on vacation at a resort hotel. He threw a beach ball to me at poolside which I managed to catch. As it turned out, I also caught him.

A fast worker, he proposed the following evening, after insisting that I put on my glasses. "For me, this was love at first sight," he said. "I want to make certain it is for you, too."

I was never a risk-taker, always careful in making decisions. It generally takes me ten minutes to decide what I'm going to wear in the morning. But I accepted Monte's proposal almost immediately. We were married four days after I graduated from college. We were very much in love and I thought our lives would be absolutely perfect forever after like in a fairy tale.

Our wedding was one I'm not likely to ever forget. You might call it unique, but then again, I'm certain other women have had similar experiences. I dreamed of the perfect wedding; however, it didn't go the way I had imagined. After the invitations went out, we started dealing with petty family problems. So-and-so wouldn't come if he or she was seated next to a particular relative. Who knew there were so many family feuds? Suddenly, we were the Hatfields and McCoys! There were also those relatives on both sides who didn't have the courtesy to respond and those that responded but then didn't bother to show up.

Then shortly before the wedding, my future hubby, a schoolteacher by profession, caught a virus from his students. I managed to come down with it the day before the wedding, which I spent alternately throwing up and shaking with chills and fever. My mother, in a panic, took me to our family doctor who jabbed me in the derriere with a double shot of penicillin. So much for being able to sit down gracefully!

Early the next morning, Mom and I had our hair done. I was feeling too sick to even have it washed. And so the hairstyle was altered a bit, sprayed so stiff it could have been used as a battering ram.

Dressed in my gown, pictures taken, I sat nervously and uncomfortably with two close friends waiting to take my fateful walk down the aisle. A waiter brought a tray of whiskey sours, but neglected to provide food. To steady my nerves, I drank a couple of rounds with my girlfriends as we waited. The trouble was I hadn't eaten anything for twenty-four hours. I might have looked svelte in my gown, owing to my enforced fast, but those drinks hit me like a freight train when I tried to stand up. My head swimming, it took all my willpower not to stagger down the aisle.

Fortunately, my head began to clear after our vows were exchanged. But strangely, the man managing our reception wouldn't allow us enter the festivities for some time. He spoke of "a slight problem." We soon discovered that our mothers had gotten into a rather loud disagreement in front of all the wedding guests. My husband's mother tried to alter the seating arrangements and my mother took exception to that. We weren't supposed to be drawn into it, but, of course, we were. It ended up being our first real argument. He supported his mother and I stood up for mine.

That evening, we finally made it to our own place. We did not have the money or the time to go on a honeymoon right away, but we had more or less furnished an apartment to live in. So there we were, finally alone, ready for our first night together as husband and wife. By then, we had kissed and made up.

I went into the bathroom to change into a sheer, sexy nightgown. I looked in the mirror and blinked. I couldn't believe my eyes. There were spots all over my face! In fact, I looked down and saw red hives all over my body! Suddenly I began to itch. Need I say, it was not the romantic night we had hoped for. We found out later that the double dose of penicillin had caused an allergic reaction.

Clearly, we didn't get off to the best start. But this turned out to be only a harbinger of bad things to come. I began teaching high school English in September. It was a difficult year, first year of marriage, first year of full time teaching. It was a period of adjustment, decidedly stressful.

That fall, just as the teaching year had gotten underway, disaster struck. It was a particularly rainy autumn. In fact, it seemed as if it never stopped raining. There was flooding everywhere. The small stream that abutted our parking lot suddenly became a monstrous, raging river.

We didn't know it when we rented the apartment, but that itty bitty scenic little stream was actually the Elizabeth River. When it flooded the parking lot of our complex, it put a few hundred cars under water. We both had relatively new cars. In fact, mine was only a few months old. My husband had expensive photographic equipment in his car as well as some beautiful sweaters and jackets. The cars were declared total losses. It took forever to get payment from our insurance company, not full value either. Meantime, we had to rent one car to share between us and it was a junker.

When I tried to explain to my school principal why I'd been forced to miss a day of school due to our situation, he exploded at me. I was new in the school and he allowed for no excuses. (His nickname was "The Enforcer"). From then on, he eyed me with mistrust and was nasty, even though the story of our flooded parking lot appeared in the local newspapers. Needless to say, it did not bode well for my longevity in my teaching position.

As to the apartment itself, living on the fourth floor of the building, we were lucky enough not to be flooded out. However, the basement and first floor were flooded. That meant that the washing machines and dryers in the basement were destroyed. The elevators no longer worked. We also lost electricity for quite some time. There were silverfish in every apartment in the complex including ours. The bad smells and dampness permeated the entire building. Mold began to form.

"It's like living in hell," Monte said.

I couldn't help but agree. Life was no longer romance and roses. The worst part was we found ourselves arguing over petty things simply because life had become very difficult for us. We were in our twenties and supposedly adults, but we really weren't fully mature.

I had never lived on my own before and so the adjustment was especially hard for me. The next school year, I worked in Staten Island, New York, as did my husband. I wasn't used to working in an urban school and found it difficult as well.

However, the worst was yet to come. In the middle of the school year, my mother was diagnosed with a terminal blood disease. As an only child who'd always had a close relationship with her mother, I was shattered, devastated.

"I don't know what to do," I told Monte. "This is like living a nightmare."

My husband took me into his arms and held me tightly. "Whatever you need to do, I'll be there to help you." And that was exactly what happened. When life was at its worst for me and I had lost hope, my husband came through with his love and support. And that made all the difference.

With Monte's blessing, I quit my job so that I could take care of my mom full time. Just as he promised, Monte helped in every possible way. He donated blood a number of times. He was kind and thoughtful to my parents. When my mother died and I cried, he was there to comfort me. He helped my father as well.

I fell in love with my husband all over again. But this time, there was nothing superficial about it. I realized something important: there is seeing and then there is truly seeing. This was not a young woman's romantic illusion. I saw my husband as he really was, and I loved what I saw. He was not perfect, but then neither was I. However, when it really mattered, my husband was there for me providing support and love. I could count on him. I guess you could call it love at second sight, and I didn't need to wear my eyeglasses to see.

From that time forward, we have always been there for each other. We both grew up. Our relationship is a fully committed one. We became better people through adversity and found a deep and abiding love. Since that time, we have faced many problems, but we have done it together. Our marriage has only gotten stronger.

Through the years, through births and deaths, joys and sorrows, our lives have been blessed by our love for each other. Recently, we have been tested again by serious health problems. We've continued to provide help, support and love for each other.

I'm very grateful that I took the risk of accepting my husband's proposal those many years ago and married him. Marriage is at best a crapshoot. I took a chance and rolled the dice. I won. Fifty years have since passed. I couldn't have chosen a better life nor would I want any other.

A Fragile Snowfall

by Patty Somlo

Moments after I told my therapist that I thought I was depressed, she gave me one of her knowing nods. Lori then explained that she believed I had suffered from chronic low-level depression, known as dysthymia, for much of my life, and occasionally dipped down into more major clinical depression.

Leaving therapy that morning, I had mixed feelings. On one level, I felt relieved. At least there was an explanation for why I felt so bad. On the other hand, I was afraid. Depression, as a psychiatric diagnosis, seemed so big. Knowing I suffered from depression with a capital D made me feel sick. Mentally sick.

A few weeks after I received my diagnosis, though, I suddenly felt more hopeful. I sensed that depression had something to teach me. I wasn't interested in taking antidepressant drugs, I knew that much, in part because I feared the still unknown long-term effects. Instead of treating symptoms, I wanted to focus on healing, from the bottom up. Or what I began calling living with depression.

Living with depression meant accepting depression in my life. For years, I had made it an almost full-time job to try and cheer myself up, from jogging to changing boyfriends and apartments, to drinking too much coffee, shopping for clothes I didn't need, and reading self-help books. Now, I knew I was depressed. I didn't have to see myself as a failure, just because I wasn't happy. It was time, instead, to get to know my depression. Time to discover what brought on the low moods and self-loathing, which too often left me feeling hopeless.

Day after day, I worked hard to pay attention to my feelings, outside of therapy, as well as within. Slowly, I began to see that when feelings such as sadness, anger, fear or shame arose, I unconsciously flicked a switch and transformed the feeling into a thought, rationalization or denial. "Oh, he didn't really mean that," or "It didn't bother me. It's no big deal." Thinking about sadness, anger, fear, and shame drained the feelings out, like wringing water from a wet cloth, and left me with the deadness I knew as depression.

Once I started paying attention, I soon learned that it was no easy task to figure out what I felt. The times I managed to recognize certain sensations, such as a tightness in my stomach I came to know as anger, I tried to go deeper, to understand what I was so angry about. I was struggling to make conscious what for most of my life had occurred under the surface of my awareness: the denial of bad feelings, which ended up leaving me feeling dead.

As I became a more careful observer of my inner worlds, I began noticing myself in certain situations suddenly become more depressed and irritated than I had been only moments before. In order to find out what caused me to become more depressed, I would trace back in my mind the events that had occurred preceding the time when my mood shifted. Then, if I was lucky, I could locate it. Oh. This person said such and such, and it made me sad.

I learned to take seriously whatever came up. Most of the time, what sparked the bad feelings seemed so minor. But the more I observed my feelings, the more I understood that I was depressed because such slight things wounded me. It was only by taking those things seriously and allowing myself to feel angry or sad that I could go deeper, to find out why such seemingly small things hurt so much.

Working with the depression in this way, I began to see that if I let myself feel, which generally meant feeling sad and crying, I could gain access to information about why I was feeling so bad. I also started to realize that I had stored up all this knowledge about my feelings and the past in my unconscious, knowledge that could help me heal, but the depression acted as a barrier to that knowledge. Feeling opened up the gates.

As I began to fear my feelings less and to experience sadness and anger and then let it go, I learned an empowering lesson: I had the ability to heal myself. Not only did I have this potential but I also understood that I carried information necessary for healing inside me.

The tool I used most to unlock the inner worlds I'd fiercely protected was the breath. In one of my first therapy sessions, my therapist taught me how to use the breath as an inner pair of eyes. With my feet planted firmly on the floor, my back straight in the chair, I inhaled and then took the breath with my mind's eye down to my feet. From there, I moved the breath up to my ankles, through the calves and knees, and on up to my belly.

This simple body check-in was like taking a hook and reeling in my mind, which loved to leap from one hopeless thought to the next. The breath pulled my mind out of the clouds and back into my body, the place where my feelings resided.

Once I learned this technique, whenever I was having trouble feeling, I planted my feet on the floor and took the breath to different parts of my body. Ninety percent of the time it worked.

Of course, it wasn't easy to experience those long-buried feelings that had built up over a lifetime. But each time I was able to let out a little of the sadness and anger — mostly by crying — I experienced a remarkable transformation. My forehead, which normally felt as if it were stuffed with tightly packed cotton, suddenly cleared, and I became happy and calm. This was the carrot I started to seek, the treat that kept me going through difficult times.

Though I was suffering a lot during this period, my therapist never made me feel that I couldn't heal. My attempts to understand the depression were met by my therapist with encouragement, validation, and applause. Each therapy session when I told her of my efforts the preceding week, she helped me believe I was on the right track. Since I kept having the experience of getting underneath the depression to relieve it, I knew I was on the right track as well.

I began to believe that I had the answers to why I suffered from depression, even if they were buried deeply within my unconscious and took time and considerable effort to unearth. The more I tried to find those answers, the more they led me to make positive changes in my life. Slowly, the life I had unknowingly built that reinforced feelings of disappointment and hopelessness, started to fall apart, brick-by-brick. In its place, I began building a healthier, more satisfying life, one that healed, rather than opened up old wounds.

Nearly seventeen years have passed since I went through that most difficult healing time. I can't say I'm cured, but neither am I miserable and hopeless, the way I was for so much of my life. The tools I acquired when I first began sitting in that straight-backed chair across from my therapist are ones I still use today. Once in a while, when too many hurts, disappointments or fears assault me at the same time, I slide back down. Unlike in the past, though, I don't fall far. Neither do I stay down for long.

Most important, I continue to experience the remarkable life transformation that living with depression has brought me. At times when my life seems the most hopeless and dark, I eventually discover what changes I need to make to pull myself back up. I understand that happiness is not a static state I will reach one day when I'm cured. Like sadness, anger, and fear, happiness ebbs and flows, and suffering causes moments of happiness to taste richer.

Many years ago when I was trying to determine if I was ready to quit therapy, I had a dream. In the dream, I was sitting alongside a sun-dappled river. The beauty of the day and the river made me so happy, I thought I might burst from joy. To hold onto that happiness for another day, I decided to make some sketches. As I sketched, a golden eagle flew past, low enough to the ground for me to touch. Seeing such a rare sight, I felt blessed. I wanted that happiness to never end.

Suddenly, the day grew dark, and I realized I had better leave the beach. As soon as I had that thought, it became so dark, I couldn't see my feet. I was forced to walk through a wall of darkness, trusting that I would somehow make it out all right.

In a few minutes, I reached the top of a sandy hill, where it was now light enough to see. When I looked to my left, I noticed it was snowing. A beautiful, light snowfall. This had been the reason for all the darkness.

When I woke up from the dream, the intensity of that happiness stayed with me, along with the sadness that it hadn't lasted. And then I realized the profound message the dream contained. Living with depression had made it possible for me to finally experience joy, and to accept the feelings of sadness when the joy faded away. I now knew that my life no longer had to be so stormy and dark, but neither would my days always be free of clouds. Most important, the dream showed me the path I needed to continue traveling, and that only by giving into the darkness and walking through it would I emerge, to see the beautiful, fragile snowfall the darkness had created.

Exit Strategy

by Avery Stiles

"Well, I have to ask, you know." My stepmom gestures to my hair, cut shorter than it had ever been. It's the beginning of October 2014, and earlier I had called my family to ask if I could stop by after my shift. I had something important to tell them.

I had worried all day before this. My roommate had assured me that I was assuming the worst, that surely I'd feel better once I told them I was planning to move away. But this is the South, with a capital "S." There are unspoken rules, lines you just don't cross.

"You know I have to ask, are you gay now or what?" Her eyes are sharp, staring at me in a way that did not grant me the permission to look away. I feel the wave building, the tension growing.

I expected more resistance when I told them I was leaving, but they seemed entirely unsurprised. At first it was smiles, assurances that they supported my decision, though they didn't agree with the timing. My degree was unfinished; I had collapsed beneath the weight of my lingering debt.

They were equally displeased that I had decided to move out west to connect with my mother's side of the family, the one they detested through a guise of pity. This I had expected, but I wasn't at all ready for what came next.

"Not gay," I say quickly, "But I feel like I have the ability to love someone no matter what they are. Man or... woman." My chest clenches, my hands feel cold.

She scoffs and shakes her head. My father struggles to hold his smile, it crumbles, curdles into something sad and painful. He hasn't said much, keeps his silence. She continues.

"I've wondered... Ever since you cut your hair, I had a feeling-"

"You said you liked my haircut when I got it."

"That was before I knew what it represented." She shakes her head again, "Have you had a 'girlfriend' yet?"

"No," I lie, but it doesn't help to quell the tsunami I see building before me.

The wave thickens with their disgust, filled with Bible verses and every reason it's disgusting to love someone of the same gender.

"They can't even have sex without using toys; it's unnatural. Do you even still believe in God?"

"Yes." I lie again. My vision is spotty and I realize I'm holding my breath.

"Stand up and look at yourself in the mirror. What on earth do you think people see when they look at you?"

I stand and I look into the mirror behind them with shame written across my face in bold lettering.

"Well? What do you think they see?"

"A... a lesbian." It's a dirty word, shameful.

"Can you see why we're concerned?" She sighs, but I can't feel their concern. I feel shame. I feel empty. Worthless.

"Come here," she beckons with a soft smile, "I think we should pray over you. We just want what's best for you, I hope you can see that. We love you so much."

I can't see it. I try to, but even as I kneel and let them lay their hands on me, their biting words from before haunting me. What are they going to tell my sisters? My grandparents would just die if they knew.

"We expected better from you. I never should have let you read all those awful books when you were a teenager..."

Prayers said, my soul hollowed out, we say our goodbyes at the door, hug, and say goodnight. They smile. I try. It seems to be enough. I go home, feeling nothing.

It takes nearly an hour for the nothingness to fade, and when it does I feel the weight of the tsunami finally come crashing down. I call Kate and tell her everything; she's in the middle of her graveyard shift, but she listens anyway. I can't stop crying, my chest feels like someone is forcing their fists inside to squeeze my heart with icy fingers.

Kate has to get back to work, and I know I should sleep. Somehow I make it to bed. Somehow I don't pick up my scissors along the way, though I hunger for the pain of their sharp edges.

I imagine my future in my head, trying to picture what lies ahead of me, but all I see is a great, black cloud. I see something going wrong, keeping me from leaving, keeping me in the dark depths of the storm with no escape.

I keep going to work, keep making myself eat every now and then. I get sick most mornings, so breakfast is no longer an option.

I start moving things around my room as if to pack, but I still didn't believe I would actually get out. While clearing off my bookshelf, my fingers touch an old boarding pass from my last trip out west, the trip that solidified my decision to leave. The paper is smooth, cleanly printed, and preserved under one of my books.

I spend a long time staring at the slip of paper, remembering the sunshine and the warm embraces of family.

Even if the waters rage around me, even if they fill me with shame and guilt until I break and overflow, there is an expiration date on the pain. I am leaving this.

I pin the boarding pass up beside my sink so that I can see it every morning, so I can remember: I am leaving this. I sell my car and start tying up loose ends. I pack. I sell the furniture I can't take with me. I reserve a van.

I remember: I am leaving this.

Thanksgiving comes, all stuffing and potatoes and tension. I remind my family that I have to work that afternoon; hotels never sleep. I leave out the fact that I volunteered for the shift so that I would have an excuse to leave before things turn ugly.

My grandparents are supposed to pick me up on their way, but my father calls to cheerily let me know that he's coming instead and will pick me up early.

I don't want this. Every holiday I remember with my stepmom begins with a tense game of mind reading and "Why haven't you done [insert task]? You know it needs to be done, why do I have to tell everyone how to do everything in his house?" up until the very moment people begin to arrive. Then the smiles and hugs turn on and the rest is shoved beneath the rug, watching and waiting until the others are gone before it rears its wretched head again.

I politely tell my dad that I'd rather go with my grandparents. "My place is on their way to yours, and they already said they would."

"Why?"

I tell him I'd just rather go with them and leave the answer at his feet. To my relief, he accepts, however reluctantly. I hate how defeated and confused he sounds. I've never really told him no before now, not like this.

Arriving at my parents' house, I feel the tsunami building all over again. The great wave rises every time I meet my stepmom's eyes. Her steely gaze thunders across the room, it makes the waves in my chest rock and crash. I make myself remember to count the days.

I'm leaving this.

The food disappears over the course of a couple hours, and I keep my eyes on the clock. It comes time to change for work, but the downstairs bathroom is occupied. My stepmom seizes the opportunity without blinking and "suggests" that I go upstairs, and I know that if I refuse, I would "cause a scene." I ascend the stairs with my uniform in hand, my stepmom close at my heels.

She corners me in what used to be my room. My gut churns, she watches me change. She closes the door and doesn't wait for me to finish undressing before she begins.

Her anger comes crashing down in waves, but for once I don't immediately crumble. I'm leaving. I'm no longer the castle of sand that falls apart beneath her surf. She berates me, but I keep my chin firm despite the tears that leak through my poorly constructed armor.

Cracked but not shattered, she brings me back downstairs to say goodbye to my family despite my still-flowing tears. I muster the least convincing smile I've ever worn, but no one questions it aloud. They hug me and let me go.

We go outside, but she can't stand my stolid silence. She demands I yell at her, says that I'll never be able to stand up for myself, that I never have and never would. I feel my own wave building within me for once. It swells as she shouts, and finally I find my voice.

My hands are white fists at my sides, my lungs empty with everything I had held inside, my wave crests and falls against her. It's nothing compared to her tsunamis, but it was a wave all my own and behind it were two words that gave it the power it needed: I'm leaving.

I tell her the only person I could never stand up to was her. I tell her I am capable of holding my own, and for once I truly feel it.

"So you're leaving because of me?" she says bitterly, arms crossed in a thorny gesture.

I don't want to lie anymore. I'm already empty, the remnants of my waves lapping tiredly at the stony shore where they'd crashed.

"That's part of it, yeah."

She nods, her eyes narrowed and her lips curled in a sick, sad expression.

My dad takes me to work. I cry most of the way there.

I spend my nights with my friends, staying close to the people whose love doesn't come with shame.

Two days before I leave, my grandparents throw a party for me. Everyone shows up, even the aunts and uncles we're lucky to see once every five years at a Christmas party. Even though they have only a couple days notice, they make the four-hour drive just to see me off.

I'm smiling all night. They ask when I'm leaving and I happily tell them. They smile, all but my stepmom, but her cold shoulder doesn't hurt me any longer.

I am leaving this.

The night dies and I say my goodbyes.

Two days later, I pack up the van, and I leave. The road greets me with open skies and endless opportunity. My tide has come in.

Hope

by Amy Lai, MD

In the summer of 1998, I had finally finished my otolaryngology residency in Boston. My daughter was born toward the last weeks of residency. A woman in a surgical residency will almost never get pregnant and take maternity leave. We were expected to show as much dedication to work as the male residents. My husband had finished his radiology training the previous year, and was working for a radiology group north of Boston. We were exhausted, but ready to start our next phase of life, as employed doctors and parents.

Our first week home from the hospital was expectedly exhausting. Not only were we new parents, but my husband Eugene was also helping his former classmates put together a "roast video" (with editing going on all night), and going to graduation parties and golf outings. In my nesting fervor, I also asked him to get rid of years of radiology journals, which he tied with twine as neat as Christmas gifts, all fifty pounds of them, and set out on the curb.

One Sunday night, as we lay with our infant daughter on the couch, watching television, Eugene suddenly felt a flutter go through his chest, and a wave of dizziness.

He got up to get a glass of water, sat down, and the flutter came again, a small bird trapped in the chest, an internal roller coaster ride. He turned to me and said, "I'm feeling a bit dizzy. Can you take my blood pressure?"

Taking blood pressure was what I had been trained to do. I was annoyed that I had gone through labor and did the majority of feeding and diaper changes at night, yet he was the one complaining of feeling weak. Get a grip, I wanted to say. Be a man.

However, his numbers were alarming. His blood pressure was low, and his heart rate was abnormally fast and weak, at 200 beats per minute, a rapid tachycardia. We discussed the next step. Possibly, the tachycardia was just from stress and caffeine, but a person in his early thirties should not react this way. Eugene thought he should be checked out in the emergency room, just to be safe. In any case, the emergency room was staffed by our friends and classmates. He would be in and out in no time. He would call me as soon as he could.

Two hours later, at midnight, he was still not home, and no one had called. I called the hospital and was transferred through to the emergency room nurse, who then said, "I'll get the doctor for you." The doctor was one of our college classmates, an old friend who was fond of practical jokes.

He got on the phone and told me, "Eugene had runs of V-tach. He's on a lidocaine drip right now and can't come to the phone. I might be able to call you in an hour or so." V-tach was ventricular tachycardia, a fast ventricular heartbeat, liable to transform into ventricular fibrillation, the state of the heart in a heart attack, in which the heart fluttered helplessly, pumping nothing.

"Right," I answered, playing along, not believing he was serious. "I'll just expect you in an hour then."

That night, I slept alone with my daughter, counting the minutes until morning, when I would bring her to the hospital with me. My husband did indeed have ventricular tachycardia, which was controlled with medications. An echocardiogram showed that the cause was something unusual: a tumor in the heart. Many tests were unable to further distinguish it as benign or malignant; it appeared to be a solid tumor. Its rarity was underscored by the lack of description in literature; a search through PubMed turned up fewer than 50 published cases. Most were malignant tumors, sarcomas. The patients with malignant tumors had an average life expectancy of six months after diagnosis, regardless of treatment.

Both of our parents came to Boston over the next three weeks, while Eugene's doctors worked to diagnose him and to discuss the best treatment. Because of the rarity of the tumor, no doctor was truly experienced in treating it; all treatment would be experimental.

Meanwhile, we waited, two people who had graduated Summa Cum Laude and Magna Cum Claude from college, helplessly waiting. Our scientific background and knowledge taunted us in their uselessness to this situation. Our baby was beautiful and astonishing, a human being with a personality from the start. She loved to be held and awoke as soon as she was put down. Her eyes were bright stars gazing just inches in front of her faces, yet she always turned to me, always vocalized when

I was near. She changed dramatically from week to week, becoming stronger, focusing more on her surroundings, completely unaware of the dramatic scenario around her.

I went through the stages of grief, unable to share them with Eugene. I awoke every day in a haze, and then, abruptly, the reality of his illness would strike me, the realest existential crisis one could have. Nature was indifferent to suffering; the world was without justice. Otherwise, how could it be that someone as intelligent, as hard-working, as full of promise as Eugene would be punished this way? What would I do without him? We were partners, had been partners for fourteen years. Could I be a good single parent? How would it change my daughter to grow up without a father?

His surgeon discussed a plan with us. He would have open heart surgery to remove the tumor. The operation would take place on a table on which radiation therapy could be given directly onto the wound, if the tumor appeared to be malignant. There was no track record for this kind of treatment, but there was only one chance to try it. The surgery was the second one of the day, and would take place in the afternoon. Afterward, he would be in the intensive care unit for a few days, intubated and sedated.

I spent a few days in the chapel of the hospital. Even though I was not a religious person, I prayed for him. I wanted to believe in the healing power of prayer. My father had told me that when he and my mother drove in from the airport, "Every traffic light was green" along the roads of Boston, a spectacular coincidence. I was a person trained in science. I did not believe in coincidences, superstitions, or the supernatural. I did not trust tele-evangelists, healers, fortune tellers, tarot card readers, or psychics. Medicine was my temple and controlled studies were my textbooks.

Still, I prayed in the silence and jeweled glow of the chapel, the fabric-covered chairs calming in their banal solemnity, the small piano correlative of the small hopes families secreted here, away from tubes and machines, from monitors and needles. I was alone with the oldest healers. Prayers are hymns from the soils of suffering people, a cry to the wilderness, seeking solace, consolation, cadence, understanding, acceptance. I prayed, not for a change in our situation, but for enlightenment. I prayed in order to strip myself of delusions, in order to live a clear-sighted life.

Faith, the pastors say, was the belief in things unseen. Faith was the opposite of proof; the "miracles" that proved divinity to man. Faith was the opposite of science. Science investigated, faith believed. What science revealed was endlessly delightful, the answer to riddles, the beautiful last piece of puzzles, the part that made the whole. Faith was perhaps foolhardy, a barbaric yawp, a lonely voice in the desert, the last prayer of the desperate.

Yet faith was what showed me, after much prayer, that life would go on, that I would survive. It was not a belief in fate or destiny as much as an acceptance that tragedy would not tear me down. Prayer showed me what I should have known, but was too distraught to see. I did not need to fake bravery. The strength was there all along, quietly waiting for me.

Here we are, eighteen years later. My daughter just started her first year in college. We have three children altogether, Eugene and I. His surgeon and treatment team were artists of the first order. The tumor was benign; he did not need any other treatment. That summer, I passed my board exam and, after a year, completed a fellowship in facial reconstructive surgery. I work as a full-time surgeon. Had the ending been different, my life would have been utterly changed. But that moment of clarity would remain, a small space in the chapel, filled with the greatest light.

My Story

by Lisa Lipscomb

In July 2012, I met my first granddaughter, named Abreeona, lovingly nicknamed Bree. On that day, I felt freedom and flight. Her presence, a breath of fresh air on that warm and sunny July day. I thought of butterflies and angels when I saw her and each time I thought about her afterward. On that day, she showed me a glowing smile. Her curly brown hair and decorative hair band accentuated the delicate lavender and white dress she wore. Dainty would easily describe her presence that afternoon. I drove two hours north to meet her with my daughter and oldest son who had previously seen her.

She and her mom lived in the city of Bad Axe, which is near the top of the "thumb" in the state of Michigan. The drive was long, but the day was bright. We passed cornfields, windmills, and small towns along the way. When we reached our destination, it was well worth it. We met on a street full of small businesses, then continued to a local park, enjoying the fresh air, breeze, and beauty of that day. Even though we'd just met, at seven months, she treated me as if she'd known me from her first day of life. All smiles! When I first became aware of her presence in this world, I asked to meet her, but was asked to wait until after a DNA test had been conducted. After seeing a photo of her, I was pretty sure she was ours. She looked a lot like me as a baby. "It's just a matter of time," I thought.

So I waited and, when confirmed, I was given her mom's contact information. I called her right away, but was sent to voicemail. I left a clear message of who I was and what I wanted. After she returned my call, we arranged to meet that weekend. I think we were all excited. Mom was looking for acceptance; I was looking forward to meeting both of them. She was nervous and didn't mind saying it. I wondered how someone I'd never met was now caring for my first granddaughter. Then I let it go. Life is filled with events we'll never be able to explain, so I take each moment as it comes. Right after we met, I was ready to schedule more visits. I also wanted our extended family to see and meet Bree and her mom, Melissa. I was ready and Melissa was open. An opportunity presented itself when my oldest grandson James celebrated his first birthday a couple months later, in September.

Bree and her mom spent that weekend at my home. It was the ideal time for them to meet more family, while celebrating her cousin's first year of life. Bree meeting our family was similar to my first experience. She was jovial and full of smiles and laughter. I've never seen a baby so receptive and free. She seemed to be comfortable with everyone she met. Her dimple and hearty, contagious laugh were noticed. What a delightful day! When she and James met that day, they were placed in the center of the dining room table, surrounded by adults. Their hello consisted of moments with them staring at one another. They were born exactly three months apart. James on September 12, Bree on December 12, 2011. After a few moments, James eyed her headband and reached for the flower on it. She smiled at him. They were a sight for sore eyes, both cute as could be. Together, a grandmother's dream.

After the party, James returned to Atlanta, where he lives. Bree returned to Bad Axe, where she resided. Then I planned more visits with Bree. As the season began to change, I was concerned about the snow and ice that would soon cover the roads between my city and hers. It would require planning, but we'd find a way to work it out. I was grateful that we'd have the opportunity to see this little girl grow up even though I missed out on her first six months.

Melissa sent pictures fairly regularly, and we planned additional visits. For her first Halloween that October, Bree was dressed up in a duck costume. I've never seen a cuter baby girl dressed in yellow. As Thanksgiving approached, we discussed sharing time. It was decided that we'd see her after the holiday and she'd spend that day with her mom up north. The night before Thanksgiving, I had a technician come to my home to repair my oven. You can't bake a turkey unless the oven is functional. My top burners worked, but I didn't want fried turkey. The repairman left momentarily for a part he needed from the local hardware store.

I smelled gas and began looking for my carbon monoxide detector. I didn't find it, but I did pick up and hold a smoke detector that was in my kitchen drawer. Without thought of why it wasn't on the wall, I continued searching for the other detector. The technician returned and I forgot about it. I began prepping for our Thanksgiving meal. I'd do the bulk of my cooking in the morning, but chopping vegetables and making dessert the night before were essential. After completing those tasks, off to bed I went. I was excited about the holiday. It was always a time when our family came together, sharing good food, great company, and catching up from our fairly busy schedules.

In the middle of the night, my phone rang. Half asleep, I looked at it, not recognizing the area code. Thinking it was someone dialing the wrong number, I rolled over and went back to sleep. If it wasn't the wrong number, surely the caller would leave a message.

I had a surreal experience that night. A feeling came over me. A sort of "ringing" or high vibration from the inside. No one else was in the room, but I heard "I am with you always." The feeling was so profound and the words clear. I knew I'd have to journal about it when I woke up. At that time, I needed more sleep. We had a long holiday in store.

Eventually, I got out of bed and after puttering around for a bit, I remembered the call from the night before. When I picked up my phone, I noticed that a message had been left, so I listened. It was an officer from Bad Axe that left a message, so I returned the call. After identifying who I was, he spoke in sentences I didn't quite understand.

There had been a fire. I asked if Bree and her mom were okay. I thought I might be driving to Bad Axe to pick them up. When he cleared up my misunderstanding, I learned that Bree, her mom, and their roommate had all perished in an apartment fire the night before.

Eventually I learned they died from smoke inhalation. I could not believe my ears. I didn't want to believe I would be able to lay my eyes on their eyes again. It felt like a Twilight Zone moment. Then I thought about my son. When asked, I requested to tell him, instead of the officer. He'd been worried about Bree lately and I knew it. I couldn't let the police call him with that news. So, I called and left him a message.

When he returned my call, I asked him to come by, it was urgent. When he arrived at my home and I opened the door, he looked at my face and literally took a step back. He recouped and entered the door, walking into the living room. He looked at me with disbelief, then grieved. I remember him saying she hadn't had a first birthday yet. He was preparing to celebrate the day she turned one.

I later asked myself what I was thinking when I agreed to break that news to him. No, I didn't want the Bad Axe police to do it, but the words that passed across my lips were words no mother should have to utter to her own child. At eleven months of age, the night before Thanksgiving, "our sweet baby" Abreeona, her mom, and their roommate died. Just as we'd started building a framework for a growing relationship, it had disintegrated by way of a fire. Our hope was snuffed out with smoke inhalation. How could this happen in a family flowing with firemen? My dad, brother, uncle, and several cousins were all firemen. This loss was even more oddly unbelievable.

One of the ministers from my church, Rev. Ric, shared words that helped with my next steps. He said, "Don't ask why, but rather what. What's next?"

So I began to focus on what I would do next. Each next step led to a decision that I could move forward with. What do we do next? A funeral and burial were planned. Bree's remains are laid to rest close to my dad's, a retired captain with the Detroit Fire Department.

When I returned to my teaching position, I became aware that many of my students didn't have smoke detectors, or they may have been missing batteries. I used social media as a catalyst to promote fire safety awareness and this urgent situation. This caught the attention of a local paper that published my story. I asked my friends and family if they had operating smoke detectors. I immediately requested that they check the batteries in their smoke detectors and touch base with family members to be sure they had done the same. I arranged for a fire safety presentation for my school and the presenter along with a host of family and friends began donating smoke detectors and batteries to my school.

Next, I distributed them to teachers who provided me with names of students who said they didn't have them. I couldn't go back and change what happened to Bree, Melissa, and their roommate, but I could reach out and help others who didn't have the properly installed equipment to keep their families safe. I was invited to present at a local school not long afterward during a community night. I framed pictures of Bree and her mom that were sure to capture the attention of passersby. My heartfelt message remains to do what you can to keep your family safe at home. Purchase and properly install smoke and carbon monoxide detectors and teach your loved ones about fire safety.

The Winter Battle

by Michelle Chalkey

I never have liked winter; its gloomy and gray skies inflicting their depressing tones upon us humans. Winter can bury us under its cold, hard snow, but only if we let it. Each year I fight a battle with nature to see whose energy is stronger.

During the winter of 2009, I lost every day.

At twenty years old, I spent the winter of my junior year in college in depression. Roommates, classmates, teachers, the busybodies of campus surrounded me, but I was completely alone and disconnected.

It started with an obsession to lose weight. I had succeeded and was on top of the world for a while, but the obsession didn't stop there. Dieting can always be restricted further. Exercise can always be pushed harder. Over time, the effects of deprivation crept up on me and sweets became my only desire. I began rebelling against the dieting industry, not realizing that I was only rebelling against myself. I failed to see my own authority in the situation.

Rebellion became the new obsession. Furious by how dieting had warped my mind, how it had forced me to overthink every crumb that entered my mouth, I wanted to eat everything I had given up. I sabotaged myself with "bad" food, hiding in my car alone to sneak embarrassing amounts of ice cream or pizza and eating until I was physically uncomfortable. When my roommates brought sweets to the dorm, I'd wait anxiously for them to go to bed so I could stuff my face with them. Several times I made brownies or cookies for other people, only to eat them in their entirety myself. The sugar became an addiction. I couldn't explain it, nor could I control it.

Every binge left me dwelling in guilt, shame, and embarrassment. I wanted to purge — rid myself of the toxins and calories — but I never physically could. Instead, I cried and shouted hateful thoughts to myself. When I saw the puffy effects the bingeing was having on my body, I hated myself more.

Each negative thought weighed down on me, and combined with the sugar overdoses left my head in a constant state of fogginess. I so badly wanted to go back to normal, but every time I buried my head in the pillow of my stiff twin dorm-room bed, I cried out more shreds of hope. One day of failure after another, I lost the shallow hope to be skinny again. I lost hope to be normal. Depression sank in, and all I could do was pray and hang on for dear life.

In the long days of winter, the blood in my veins seemed every bit as dead as the limbs of the trees. Detrimental thoughts swarmed in my head like vicious, cold gusts of wind knocking me around and sucking the life out of me. Slow, quiet tears fell down my cheeks night after hopeless night in sync with the snowfall.

In the dead of winter, I waited for that one day when the sun would shine and zap energy into my being again. All I had to do was let its rays hit me, and pray that they would do the work to make me normal again.

Yet, various forms of sunshine forced their light on me throughout my depression; I just couldn't always feel them.

One ray of light came in the unconditional love of my mother. Although she couldn't relate, she provided a non-judgmental ear for listening and open arms for crying. Mom called me every day that winter. Sometimes she'd ask how I was doing, and other days she simply reminded me that she and my dad loved me. Although her positive messages seemed small and quiet in comparison to the overbearing echoes of my negativity, their consistency expanded my capacity for hope.

But Mom knew she could only help so much. She encouraged me to seek counseling at my campus, which offered free services for students. I met with a female counselor once a week, and no one but my mom even had to know about it. Each session, I cried and told my counselor of my feelings of unworthiness, my struggles of bingeing and getting back to my skinny self, my fear that I would never be able to return to my normal lifestyle. The counseling sessions provided the alone time that I needed to speak of and process everything that brought me to depression. She helped me understand that the goal wasn't to go back to normal, but to move forward to the real me. Who I referred to as my skinny self was someone who lived by the judgment of others. I needed to move forward and start living for my true desires.

I did have something to look forward to at the end of the spring semester. Before depression came in, I had signed up for a theater class that would allow me to travel to London for two weeks in May 2010. Traveling abroad had always been a dream of mine, and school presented a wonderful and educational way to do it. The trip, however, would also be out of my comfort zone. I'd be traveling with new people and teachers that I'd meet in class. I wouldn't have my mom or anyone I knew well enough with me to pick me up if I broke down.

In my first week of this class, I didn't think I'd be able to do it. The theater students were a unified group of confident and self-assured people. They spoke loudly and confidently with intense beauty, but they also came in all different shapes and sizes. They had their own physical flaws, but they didn't hide behind them the way I did. They didn't fear their weight or see it as anything to be ashamed of. They were proud of who they were, and it inspired me. I had so much to learn from them, but I felt like an outsider watching it all. While I was naturally shy before, the depression and binge eating had taken away any confidence I had left. I couldn't speak up and fit in with this group.

The theater students didn't know of my problems. They didn't know if my quiet, sad personality was my character or if something deeper was going on. But they helped me more than they can possibly know.

I could have quit the theater class. I could have quit counseling. While I couldn't see the good in any of them at the brink of my depression, my mother told me to keep getting out and going anyway. Week after week, my depression would go up and back down, showing no real progress. But the steady, consistent act of showing up each week, of being exposed to these gifts of energy, slowly built up the positive effects they had on me.

As the snow cleared that spring and the trees began rebirthing new leaves, positive energy ran through me again, slowly at first, gaining more speed with each day. By the time the trip to London came around, I felt more comfortable around the theater students. I saw the opportunities for a fun and new experience with them overseas. I was able to talk to my mom and my counselor without crying. What's more, I left my last counseling session utterly happy and excited for my trip. And I came home from London with immense joy and confidence and a handful of new friends.

Losing hope is scary. When you feel you've exhausted all of your energy into what brought you down, it seems impossible to climb back up and move on to a happy, normal life. The single most important thing that helped me was having someone to talk to without judgment. I was lucky enough to have my mother checking in with me every day.

Although she couldn't quite relate or understand my pain, she cared about helping me. She listened to me. If you have someone like that in your life, go to them. That one person will keep you going and give you someone to want to get better for. If you don't have this person in your life, gather all the strength you can to seek help. See a counselor or therapist. No matter who it is, having someone to talk to keeps you from being entirely alone in your own head during a challenging time. I always left counseling sessions feeling lighter, with slivers of hope, knowing I'd return the following week no matter what.

Keep showing up for the routine things in your life. The first time you miss something due to depressive thoughts, the more likely you are to miss again. During my depression, I kept going to class. This was the best way to keep some sense of normalcy in my life.

Whether or not you're battling depression, make a point to see your strengths every day and acknowledge them. Make a daily practice of believing in yourself and seeing the beauty and positivity in the world even on the dark and gloomy days. Do this, and depression will be easier to fight off when it tries to come back.

Do things you enjoy. Play, color, stretch. Move your body in ways that are fun. In my case, it was important not to see this as needing to do vigorous exercise, but to get blood flowing and energizing the body.

The dark seriousness of this experience left me fearing for much of my twenties that I would fall back into it. I've largely overcome this fear now, almost seven years later, but certain triggers occur almost daily that remind me of that dark time. Now I work on strengthening my mind, spirit, and body throughout the year to be mentally tougher should dark days come around again. I know now that I have the ability to see the light in every shaded situation. By constantly lifting myself up even when things are good, I make it harder for anything to bring me down.

The seasons will change every year. Winter will come again. Let's learn to fight the battle before it's here, so that when it comes, we'll already be winning.

Three Strikes and I'm *Back!*

by S.K. Naus

In my background, people usually held one job at one company until retirement. Those who were ambitious would get into a company on the bottom rung and then slowly, over the years, work themselves up to a good position from which they would eventually retire. So when I finally completed my higher education and landed a good job with a good company, I believed that this was my path also. Wow, was I ever wrong!

The first time I was laid off, it was like I'd just been hurled off a cliff: one day my job was there and the next, it was gone! And since I'd been with the company for nearly a decade and had settled in so well that I was actually able to visualize my own retirement party, the hurt was that much worse.

You can't begin to imagine my shock when I was given abrupt notice. It was as though I'd entered an alternate reality where I had suddenly become a pariah no one wanted around. I was stunned at the security detail on-hand and speechless at the way the now ex-employees were escorted to their desks to pick up their belongings before being led out of the building never to darken that doorstep again. The moment I got home, I burst into tears. The pain of rejection was overwhelmingly raw and fresh. How could someone treat me like I was poop on the bottom of a shoe? I was appalled and ashamed. I was also embarrassed that something like this had happened to me.

How was it possible to be a valued and respected employee one second and then treated like a possible criminal element the next? People kept telling me it wasn't personal and that in no way was this my fault but deep down I was extremely hurt and angry. Why me? Yes, that pathetic refrain kept whirling through my mind till I thought I'd go crazy trying to figure it out. The bottom line was that it had happened and now I had to deal with it.

The company offered what was called "life management" classes to all the redundant employees. I quickly learned it was really just therapy on how to cope with the difficult situation and how to market yourself for a new position. Another laid-off employee convinced me to go with her as the month-long course had prepaid for each one of us. I'm glad I went as not only did we become fast friends, we helped each other over this hurdle and bolstered one another's spirits when facing job interviews.

Fortunately, I was still young and eventually regained my confidence. I managed to find another job, one closer to home this time. It was at a small satellite office of a much larger company and I was there for five years when suddenly that same axe fell on me. Again, I was targeted. Once more, I was filled with hurt and anger. There had to be something wrong me that I was so mercilessly picked on. Why was the bullseye always on my back? What had I done to deserve this? This second rejection stung woefully and I felt such a dark dreary cloud hanging over me.

The bitter aftertaste stayed with me for quite a while. I just couldn't seem to shake it. At this point in time, I also felt a great embarrassment to have to include "lay off" for a second time on my revised resume. Each time, I went to an interview, I mentally crossed my fingers that these two strikes would not be counted against me and that the company would see me as the asset I really could be to them.

It also frightened me to realize this was now a much younger workforce I was competing in. I remember going into one interview wearing a skirt and blazer with hose; the style made me feel like an office professional. But when I left, I saw a couple of candidates waiting in the reception area simply wearing sweaters with slacks and bare feet in sandals. It made me feel out of the loop and in need of a wardrobe change. How was I ever going to get another job?

Not long afterwards, a two-week assignment miraculously morphed into a permanent fulltime job. I was thrilled about it, especially since this third job was even closer to home. I was happy there and met someone with whom I am still fast friends. But the winds of change suddenly blew over this company when new management was brought in. The once rosy work atmosphere disappeared and I sensed foreboding changes ahead. Sadly, I was right.

After this third layoff, I held it together till I reached home where I curled up into a ball and cried my heart out at yet another rejection. I just couldn't believe how this could happen over and over. It was like a cycle and I badly wanted to break it. I began to blame myself and needed time to lick my wounds. Surely this had to mean there was something wrong with me. I was defective in some way and that was the reason employers kept showing me the exit door. I questioned my skills, my qualifications, my experience and myself in general. There was a lot of wasted time spent on self-pity and self-analysis.

But time lessens the hurt and I was able to pick myself up, dust myself off, and go out on another job search. This time around, it seemed much harder and I refused to admit that age had anything to do with it; but, just going to interviews confirmed I was usually the oldest of the applicants. And there were always many applicants.

It was at this particular time in my life that I picked up a popular book I'd heard about years earlier entitled *The Secret*. I remember the author had appeared on an episode of the famous Oprah Winfrey show and the book had been highly touted as a realistic common sense approach to self-help. I wondered to myself if this little book could make a difference to me in some way.

For the last couple of years, I'd been working on an assignment basis and I used to carry everything in a tote bag from one company to the next because I could never really make myself at home anywhere. How could I? I wasn't a permanent employee and assignments were not always extended or renewed. I decided to buy the book and found myself unable to put it down.

I read the book from cover to cover and then re-read it again. I kept asking myself how I had become so blind that the simple things listed in the book had escaped my sight. I felt like a child again, having to re-learn all of these basic lessons I had somehow forgotten. I was in awe of some of the examples showing how people had been able to change their lives by adapting what they'd read in this book to themselves. It was in a word: amazing. The best part was that it all made sense. I finally regained clarity!

Even during my initial reading of the book, I immediately began to readjust my train of thought as well as my attitude. I found I was actually liking myself again and it helped me to find my self-worth that had somehow become beaten down over the years. It opened my eyes to the fact life is all about give and take and balance. I developed recognition that I was not only valued but had purpose. I counted!

Immediately after I started reading the book, I was on a job listing site and saw an opportunity literally at the next intersection from where I lived. It was the last day for the listing and instead of thinking it was too late and one more application would just be forgotten, I composed a cover letter and sent it in with my resume. The following week, I was called for a panel interview; the next week, I joined the company on what turned out to be a three-year contract. I was elated! I knew in my heart it was an accomplishment and not simply a stroke of luck.

The book is now a part of my life. If I'm not reading it, I read *The Power* or *Hero*, the two subsequent books by the same author. I find them to be profound and never tire of them. When my job ended, I was already preparing myself for something better and I was able to start another contract as summer replacement elsewhere. Again, I enjoyed the work and, after several months, was hired on a permanent basis.

Family and friends are the best support system to have when surviving a layoff. But if more motivation and assistance is needed, a self-help book is an inexpensive form of therapy and guidance I'd recommend. It enabled me to see my situation objectively and resolve the subsequent issues and emotions prompted by unexpected job loss.

Now I can say not only am I glad I bought the book, I'm glad it helped me find my way back to myself again!

Lessons Learned

by Beatrice Hogg

In August 2008, I left a stressful full time job with the California Department of Social Services in Sacramento, California, confident that I would quickly find a new job. I had worked steadily since my first job as a welfare caseworker for the Commonwealth of Pennsylvania in 1980. A few months later, the economic downturn hit. In November 2008, I went to sign the papers to start a job as a counselor at a local community college. Before I could sign the papers, I was told that the job had been eliminated that morning. I was devastated. Little did I know that I would not have a full-time job again until July 2015.

I worked a part-time job at the college for six months until budget cuts eliminated that position. I received unemployment insurance benefits and federal extensions until I exhausted all funds in September 2011. Even though I applied for lots of jobs, no one would hire me. Government hiring had stopped, but my civil servant background made me unemployable. Potential employers told me that I "wouldn't be happy here," because of my former government salary. I told one employer, "I would be happy not to have to receive food stamps." Because I didn't have a car, local non-profits wouldn't even offer me a job because I would be expected to transport clients in a personal vehicle. One potential employer said, "If you get a car in the next week, call me back." How was I supposed to afford a car, when I could barely pay my rent? After the unemployment ran out, I was no longer to even do that. One week before Christmas, I was evicted from my apartment of ten years.

The only offer I had for housing was from an acquaintance in Berkeley whom I had only known for a few months. I put some of my belongings in a small storage unit, but most of my things ended up in the dumpster the night before I left my apartment. Because I had no one to help me, I left all of my furniture behind. A beautiful desk, bookshelves, most of my bedding and linen, chairs, tables, dressers; all gone. The next morning, another friend drove me to the house in Berkeley. I quickly learned that I had made a mistake. My acquaintance was a hoarder with mental health problems, who assigned me the floor of a dirty, cold room in the back of her cluttered house. Even though I hung them up every day, the room was so cold that my bath towels never completely dried. After two weeks in a toxic environment in Berkeley, I got an Amtrak ticket for my birthday. I went to Los Angeles on my 55th birthday to stay with a friend. Once I got there, she rescinded her offer. After spending two nights at a hostel (a birthday gift from a friend in Pennsylvania), I was at Venice Beach, waiting with fifty other people for the homeless bus to take me to the emergency winter shelter. From January until April 2012, I was homeless on the streets of Los Angeles.

In April, a friend in Sacramento offered me a room in her house. I stayed with her and her family for three years. It was hard to live with a family that wasn't my own and even harder to live by someone else's rules. I had been on my own since I was 18, and living with other people at 55 was so stressful that my hair started falling out. During that time, I continued to look for work while receiving welfare and food stamps. I started a blog to write about the things that I experienced, as a way to keep myself sane. After I was featured in a *New York Times* article about long-term unemployment, I decided to write about the lessons I learned from my experiences.

1. Have friends who are going through similar struggles.

In my life, I have Mary, Lorraine, Teresa, Dorothy, and Deb. Without them, I probably would have killed myself or someone else a long time ago. Believe me, people who have not been unemployed during this economic downturn *do not* understand what you are going through. And long-term unemployed people over fifty have special issues these days that younger people do not have to deal with. The combination of less jobs, jobs that don't pay a living wage, employer reluctance to hire older, long-term unemployed persons, the requirement of specialized skills instead of general knowledge, and many other factors make this recession vastly different from the ones that have occurred previously. If you don't have any friends you can commiserate with, talk to people at your nearest job search center, connect with people online, even if you just leave comments on websites like the National Employment Law Project (www.nelp.org). As long as you get confirmation that you are *not* alone. But if you feel that your mental health issues go beyond feelings of inadequacy or frustration because of your lack of employment, seek professional help. Call a suicide prevention hotline if you feel that you might harm yourself. Many cities have mental health clinics or places set up for low income persons to get treatment. Don't be afraid to ask to help.

2. Treat yourself.

Sure, funds are limited and times are tough, but do something that makes you feel good. Even if it is just taking a walk, going to a free museum, a free event, or joining friends for a cup of coffee, you need to find some joy in your life. I wouldn't recommend spending your last dollar in a thrift store or on the lottery, of course, but do what you need to do. Remember: every day that you wake up is a good day.

3. Learn from your mistakes and don't dwell on the past.

Everyone who has been affected by the economic downturn would probably have done things differently if they had known what was on the horizon. But you can't beat yourself up about it. You can't change the past, but you can learn from it. I never in a million years thought that I would end up homeless, but it has given me insights that I would never had gotten any other way. Everything is a learning experience... blah, blah, blah. As Mary always says, "It is what it is."

4. Find your passion.

There has to be something that you wanted to do or try that you never had the time for or the balls to do before. Look into things that inter- est you. Go to a lecture on the subject, take some community college or community center classes, hang out at places where people do what you want to do. Maybe once you see it from the inside, you will discover that it isn't for you. But a lot of times, you have to step out of your com- fort zone. Maybe people won't take you seriously because you are older or inexperienced. But check it out anyway. All they can say is "no" and that won't kill you. I'm not one for taking giant leaps, but little baby steps may be all you need to get the ball rolling.

5. Don't give up.

Even though the *New York Times* says, "The long-term jobless, after all, tend to be in poorer health, and to have higher rates of suicide and strained family relations." (Lowrey, Annie. "Caught in Unemployment's Revolving Door." *New York Times*. N.p., Nov. 17, 2013; Web. Nov. 17, 2013.) But don't let it get you down for long. Sure, everyone has those days when you just want to throw a giant pity party and stay in bed. But don't stay there indefinitely. Good things do happen and sometimes they actually happen to good people. People laugh when I tell them that I enter lots of contests. But in the last year, I have won a VIP trip to Los Angeles (which included airline tickets, transit passes, restaurant vouchers, museum and amusement park passes and a $500 gift card), CDs, concert tickets, tee shirts and other stuff.

Other than writing contests, I only enter contests that have no fees attached. I read the general rules and make sure that it is legitimate. Be careful who you give your personal information to, though. Entering contests is fun and it gives me something positive to think about for a while. And that never hurt anybody.

I have always found that in my life, "Truth is stranger than fiction." So don't give up. Be proactive rather than reactive. I can't say that I believe in a fairy-tale happy ending, but I believe that moments of happiness happen in all of our lives.

In the fall of 2014, a former co-worker told me about a civil service test being given for a social work position with Sacramento County. We both took the test and in July 2015, I was hired as a social worker for the Department of Human Assistance, helping families on welfare who were experiencing homelessness or domestic violence. I tell my clients about my experience with homelessness and long-term unemployment to give them the confidence and support to improve their own lives. In November 2015, I moved into my own apartment. Even though there were times that I thought about giving up, I kept going. My experiences and the lessons that I had learned have made me stronger.

If I could survive that, I can survive anything.

Thanks Be to God

by Ruth J. Hartman

Several years ago, something happened to me. Something terrible. Unexpected. Devastating. The kind of disaster you think you'll never recover from. When I was 27, I was working as a dental hygienist in our small rural community. The job had always been painful physically for my hands and back, and stressful mentally and emotionally, but I was at least coping and the job had gone along fairly well.

Until, it didn't.

Strange thoughts struck me so suddenly, so harshly, I was nearly brought to my knees in fear. Doubt. Confusion. It was as if some alien had taken over my mind. And I couldn't make it leave.

You've probably heard someone say, "I have OCD." (Obsessive Compulsive Disorder.) Or maybe you have it. I think every person may have a little bit. They obsess over whether a tidy house, precisely hung pictures, an even number of green beans on their plate. Or count the steps as they go upstairs. Thankfully for most people, it's seen as a quirk, an oddity. Something to joke about. Well, mine wasn't.

One day while I stood cleaning the dental operatory after a patient had left, I suddenly felt inadequate to the task. Something I'd done repeatedly several times a day for years — making sure my operatory was sufficiently prepared for the next person — now wasn't enough. Had I been paying close enough attention to what I was doing, or was I already contemplating the supplies I would need for my next patient on the schedule?

What if I didn't get every single surface of every single appliance, chair, and counter, clean? If I missed the tiniest, most minuscule area on the underneath side of the chair arm, the indentation on the cord of my hand piece, the narrow ridge on the top of my patient tray handle. Could a germ, something unseen yet dangerous, something deadly, be left behind to infect the next person who came in? Patients who put their trust in me to do my best for them, to keep them safe? Who only intended on coming to me for a cleaning, not leave with some unwanted disease?

I couldn't shake the image. It wouldn't let me go. It plunged its wicked, sticky little fingers deep into my brain, saying over and over and over, "What if you missed something? What if something bad happens, because of you?"

Because of you…

The guilt was heavier than any I'd ever known. The fear of it nearly paralyzed my mind. I couldn't bear the possibility that I might be somehow responsible for another person's ill health; me, a health professional, a specialist in my field, a person who cared about the wellbeing of those I treated.

My thoughts jumped from patients possibly catching a common cold germ, to the spread of flu and pneumonia, finally landing on the one thing that terrified the world: AIDS. If someone contracted that disease because of my negligence, I didn't think I'd ever recover from the crushing guilt.

When all of this occurred, it was in the early nineties, when news stories about AIDS were prevalent. When gossip and fear and even reported news stories got it all wrong. People were desperate to avoid the illness, to the point of needlessly ostracizing those poor souls who'd ended up contracting it. We'd studied the disease in class, so I knew the facts. Knew that it was highly unlikely that someone would ever, could ever, get AIDS in that fashion, but what if the facts I'd learned were wrong? The wild new thoughts, bound together in a formidable tight knot that wouldn't leave me alone.

My hands shook. And my legs. My body ran hot then cold. But I kept cleaning. Sterilizing. Making sure I hadn't left anything on the equipment that wasn't supposed to be there. I glanced over to my cabinet that held all of my instruments. They were clean, weren't they? What if I'd forgotten to have them sterilized? Or the autoclave had malfunctioned and though they appeared clean, they still had germs on them? I had to know for sure. Guilt tore at me, because what if because of my mistake, or failure of our equipment caused a patient to suffer? Or die?

It was too much. The guilt. The worry. The fear. I was stuck in an endless loop of questions with no answers. I didn't understand why this was happening to me, but whatever the reason, something new and hideous had moved into my head. The whole time these thoughts wreaked havoc in my mind, I kept right on disinfecting, even when I glanced at the clock and saw that I was running late.

But when I heard footsteps coming from the hall, I knew I had to hurry. My boss didn't like to run behind, even a few minutes. I tried, I really did, but I just kept on cleaning. He stopped in the doorway, and frowned. Knowing his temper and the fact that I really needed the job, I abandoned my scrubbing. I told him I was almost ready. With a scowl, he passed on by. Thankfully.

I'd hoped the strange thoughts — obsessions, I soon realized — would go away. Instead of fading into the darkness quietly, they intensified, came more frequently, and plagued me so much that soon, I couldn't do my job. I begged for time off work, telling my boss the reason was because of carpal tunnel. While it was true I had pain in my hands, it was just a convenient excuse. He knew the real reason though. He'd confronted me one night after work and pointed out that he thought I had OCD. By that point, I knew it too. I'd taken enough psychology classes to know the signs. Still, having him come right out and say it made it real.

I was off for months, fending off my boss' weekly phone calls asking when I was coming back. Finally, I just quit. It was all I could do to just survive each day and force myself out of the house for my weekly appointments with a psychiatrist. There was no way I could go back to seeing patients, acting like nothing was wrong, and putting myself through even more torture than I faced in my own house. Because the thoughts didn't end once I left the dental office as I'd hoped. They just followed me wherever I was, with whatever I did, merrily destroying my sanity. My husband was very supportive. I wouldn't have made it through without him. Even now, I ask him why he didn't have me committed to a hospital — because believe me, he had reason — but he just shakes his head. Says he wouldn't have done it. That he loved me too much to see that happen.

Along with my husband, my family and close friends were a huge part of what got me through every day. Though I knew they grew tired of it, they all patiently listened to me talk about what was happening in my mind, my inability to complete even the simplest task for fear of doing the wrong thing, not doing something well enough. Causing harm to myself or others through my actions or failure to act. The most frightening phase of it all, though, was my hallucinations. I'd see blood where there was none. I'd think I'd done some unspeakable thing to myself or others.

And the worst, when I saw — actually saw — a man sitting in my living room. I can even remember that hallucination to this day. What he looked like. What he wore. That he had crooked teeth and long, bony fingers. To say I was terrified was an understatement.

The man hadn't really there, of course. And I hadn't done any of the things I was convinced I had. But to me they were real, true, and factual. All of this lasted, growing progressively worse, for over four years. I'd given up hope of ever seeing the end of it, outside of death, which I contemplated often. The most frightening thing I've ever encountered, even worse than the fear and hallucinations, was a deep-seated doubt that God even existed. I'd been a Christian since the age of nine. But now, I wasn't sure if He was even real. I tried to imagine Him, but there seemed to be some sort of wall in my mind. A barrier that kept me from knowing. I couldn't get past the thought that maybe my whole life, my belief in God, my father's weekly sermons in our church, were all lies.

But I was healed.

My healing came from God through way of medication. After a failure of one drug to give me any relief, my doctor and I hit upon success. Prozac. It melted away my anxiety, dissolved thoughts that got stuck in a continual loop and wouldn't stop, and quieted my certainty that I'd done something harmful. Not that I don't still have OCD. I do. Always will. And when I'm stressed, sometimes the thoughts reoccur. But, thanks be to God in giving me the medication, it's controllable. Bearable. Livable.

Yes, thanks be to God.

The Beginning Starts with the End

by Robyn Alezanders

I became something I never thought I would, a victim of domestic abuse, and in addition to years of terror, also went through an abortion. But I also became a survivor.

I had a kindergartener and a toddler, and knew I was done having children. Yet the decisions about children, and about sex in general, were not entirely mine. The man who called himself my partner, who had long ago lost my love and trust, was now just the monster who would not let me leave, not let me live my life without him. Sex was either at his demand and bullying, or something to try to appease him and hold off his terroristic threats as best as possible. It was as impersonal as it could be, just as it had been from the very beginning: no kissing, no foreplay, just pushed down and lay there until it was over, faking enjoyment to hopefully prevent a tirade of what was wrong with me. And naturally, there was no birth control.

I found out I was pregnant when he was staying at his mother's, after yet another round of hell that looked like it was going to be become yet another restraining order (which I would dismiss, believing his "I'll change" pleas). Funnily enough, I had recently ended a period, but the period was strange; very light in color and flow, and just not feeling right. I was peeing all of the time, my boobs hurt, I was extraordinarily tired, and juggling ravenous hunger and dizzying nausea. Having gone through pregnancy before, despite the odd bleeding, suspected the worse, and bought a dollar store test. I couldn't afford buying the drug store one, and figured I already knew the answer anyway. Sure enough, the two lines popped up quicker than me spilling out the cup of extra urine in the toilet.

The affirmation was extremely conflicting. I didn't want any more children with him, yet had ambivalent feelings about termination. I was pro-choice, yet here was the ultimate test of that stance. At the core of why I still remained in this heavily toxic and at many times dangerous situation, was that I was financially stuck; I did not have the money to take my kids and leave, and sustain the three of us by myself. I was also emotionally and psychologically broken-down, believing that as his daily taunts were, that no one would ever want me, that I was a nothing, and destined to always be alone. Having this baby would further tie me to this abuse, and its conception was more than just the result of not using birth control, it was the result of sex that was not mutually desirable or genuinely wanted.

Creeping in my brain though, was an insidious whisper that I also didn't want my last pregnancy to be a termination, that that's not how I wanted my memories and account of my life to be. But with an extremely heavy heart and spot on my soul, I deemed it best to go through with ending it.

It was a three-day process at the clinic. First, I had to have the pregnancy confirmed, then I had to attend an orientation of sorts, where everything was explained, and then the actual procedure. I had to take my kids with me the first day, and what an experience that was: spending hours in a reception room, placating two youngsters with snacks, toys, and books, while waiting to hear that yes, indeed there was a developing embryo that I needed to schedule the end of. The time between that day and the orientation was surreal. I gave in to cravings, indulging in the extra food my body was demanding, and remained Mommy of The Year to my boys, all the while obsessively researching the procedure online, whether or not to choose surgical instruments or a pill to terminate, and what to expect afterwards. Other than telling him (because I had been mostly cut-off from everyone; he and his family were still my main source for assistance with the kids), this entire swirl of emotions and decisions were kept to myself. I had no other outlet.

To a certain degree, I put everything in the back of my mind, knowing what had to be done, and yet looking at it from a disconnected point of view. Every time I used the bathroom or felt a twinge, I hoped for a miscarriage, for that would have been easier to deal with.

The second day at the clinic proved to be even more surreal. All women contemplating scheduling the procedure had to sit in a room together and watch a video explaining everything. There was also a nurse and counselor present to answer any questions. When we were told that the procedure was only done on certain days, and that it meant arriving first thing in the morning and being there for a full day, many of the women began loudly protesting. They had hair and nail appointments to get to, places to go, plenty of other things apparently that this appointment would inconvenience them with. I know that people have different ways of dealing with things, and some try to incorporate humor or some other kind of distracting tactic (I myself wasn't entirely grieving, yet), but the majority of reactions around me were disconcerting.

He took me to dinner the night before, to a local diner, where I gorged on a greasy cheesesteak and onion rings; one of the last times I ate meat. He tried to have sex with me that evening, but luckily, I was able to tell him no, without an explosion. The Friday my pregnancy officially ended, I recall walking through protestors trying to block the entrance, fighting off the urge to try to get them to understand why this was the best decision for everyone, and that this day was far from the worst in my life. I remember a counselor asking me if I had a support system, and me telling her that yes, indeed, I did, biting my lip to divulge the truth. I still see the nurses in the room, the one holding my hand and talking about my visible tattoos as a way to keep me focused, the butterfly stencils on the room's ceiling, and I will always associate Tori Amos' "Give," with being the first song I heard on my iPod as I lay in recovery.

I spent the weekend at his mother's house, dozing in the armchair in the living room. I think the only thing I forced myself to eat was take-out sweet and sour soup. And then it was back to my "normal" life, with him now also returning to the home again, for yet another cycle of "being better."

Monday morning, he went to work, and I dropped my older son off to school, and then spent the day with my younger son. I tried not to think about everything, just put it in my head I was simply having another period, every time I changed pads and took another dose of painkillers. That afternoon, I picked up my son, made dinner, and carried on as usual, going through the motions, and even having civil, simple talk with him.

The next day, it hit. A couple of hours after taking my son to school, as my other son napped, I broke down in the kitchen, just dropped to the floor and cried long and hard, unleashing all of the anger and pain from not only the immediate loss of this baby, but the loss of me, that had been systemic for far too long. I didn't know how long I could carry on this new phase of pretending everything was all right, and knew I could no longer go through this battle alone.

Although I was still under the same roof as him, and still had to endure a lot until I was finally able to take my kids and leave, I started the steps that would eventually help lead to my confidence in doing so. I found free counseling services that not only addressed the grief in my loss, but also how to deal with him while I was still stuck, and how I could begin developing exit strategies. The counselor was part of a Christian-based organization that encouraged women to keep or adopt out their babies rather than abort them, but were support services for babies lost to stillbirth, miscarriage, or where an abortion was still done. My spiritual beliefs were as far from Christian ideology as possible, but I needed someone who was specifically trained in dealing with this kind of loss, and I expressed so at our first session. The therapist was very gracious and respectful of our personal differences, became a wonderful source for talking, listening, and revealing everything to. She was one of the first people that I was able to not remain quiet and "everything is fine" with.

Shortly after the abortion, I noticed butterflies more than usual, landing on me and flitting about, and an echo of what was in the surgical room. As much as the sadness and despair filled me, and as much as I wanted to forget, I also wanted to do something that still acknowledged a part of it. I got a tattoo of a fairy with butterfly wings, an image that will always hold a private essence as to its meaning.

These were huge steps that effectively made a difference. Grieving an abortion doesn't have to be synonymous with any particular belief system, and I'm grateful that I gave the therapist a chance, and that she respected my own beliefs enough to put aside her own, and to be receptive to hearing how I applied mine to this occurrence in my life. Putting a more concrete aspect to the loss was also monumental. It doesn't have to be a tattoo; it could be a piece of jewelry, a journal entry, a piece of art, whatever speaks to the heart and keeps it from being locked away to build up even more pain. And if there is anything else connected to it, such as domestic abuse, taking the scariest jumps of all to put an end to it is fundamental, vital to a new journey.

I still occasionally think about how old the baby would have been now, if it would have been a boy or girl, even if I could have still found a way to finally leave and still have him/her. He/she became the leap to getting out, and so in a way, will always be with me.

The Return

by Kyra Harsh

I stood before my husband, wide-eyed and shivering, twisting his itchy wool sweater tightly around my fingers and softly pleaded, "Save me from myself." There was no hero. There was no savior or knight in shining armor coming to whisk me away on his white horse. The man I loved could not even save me. I was my own worst enemy and at the exact same time, my own liberator. I was the one I was waiting for.

Let's rewind approximately eight weeks. My husband and I sat on our back porch as he received a phone call stating that his uncle had passed away that afternoon. I silently watched as he collapsed and wept. Uncle Prep was the patriarch of the family, someone who had been there for my husband his whole life and the other half of a couple we both admired so dearly. What would the world be like without this man? I felt sadness and yet I wouldn't let myself cry. More than anything I felt the need to be strong for my family.

A few days later we arrived at the funeral services. It would be my first funeral, at 29 years old. We entered the back of the room as Uncle Prep lay at rest in his casket in the front of the room and I could barely look. I'm no stranger to the deceased as I had been communicating with passed souls for about 20 years by that point. I offered condolences as I hugged Prep's daughter, son, and then finally his wife. I turned around and stared at the body for what seemed like an eternity and all of the sudden my knees went weak and I felt my body start to shake. I grabbed onto my husband for balance and through my embarrassing explosion of tears I said, "Get me out of here." This is when I realized, "being strong for the family" is a complete sham.

It sounds cliché but there is no better way to put this other than: one day I woke up and things were not the same. The next few days I didn't feel right, or felt out of it, and very quickly and agonizingly I began analyzing every single aspect of my life, and that is no exaggeration.

Just a few of the questions I constantly asked myself were, What is the point of all of this? What is my purpose and why am I here? Am I really here or is this just a dream? Do I deserve to be here? What if I died right now? What if I had some horrible disease? What if I feel "out of it" for the rest of my life? What if I committed suicide? What if I felt like I wanted to hurt my children? When will I stop thinking this way? What if I'm going crazy? I had nearly lost all hope for a better tomorrow.

I have had the challenge of anxiety and depression from a relatively young age. I suffered from my very first panic attack when I was 12 years old during the facial transplant portion of the movie *Face Off*. For those of you not familiar with the movie, it was gruesome. I had to squash my face against the screen of my living room window because I thought I wasn't getting enough air and I couldn't breathe.

It might be worth noting that I have also had the challenge of adapting to everyday life as an empath. I had a horribly abusive childhood, a narcissistic mother, a co-dependent father, and moved across the same ocean twice before I was six. Needless to say, my way of coping with life's overwhelming times had been less than conducive to maintaining my version of sane.

During this time, there was a solid two weeks that I began every day, sometimes before my eyes would even open in the morning, with a panic attack. I was utterly afraid of the day and the potential invasive thoughts that might come my way. I spent the better part of October 2015 in an almost constant state of depersonalization and debilitating anxiety. People genuinely scared me, the outdoors scared me, and I scared myself.

One night, in the midst of a looming panic attack, I decided to reach out to one of the women I work with, Jacquie. We worked together in a chat room and I had always considered her a mentor of mine. With Jacquie's help, it became more and more apparent to me that I needed to reassess, relearn, and practice new techniques when it came to my anxiety. Jacquie's biggest message to me was, "You are human," and that, as simple as it sounds, was exactly what I needed to hear.

A huge part of suffering with anxiety and panic is patterning. One of my sisters, for instance, would begin to experience anxiety every time she got in the car to drive and it became a habit for her to associate anxiety and/or panic attacks with driving. Those of us who suffer start to anticipate the anxiety before it even begins which, in turn, causes anxiety! I refer to it as "having anxiety about having anxiety." For me, simply the time of day was a trigger for me, as mentioned before with my morning anxiousness. It was also around 9 p.m. at night, after the all the kids went to bed, that I would find myself wrapping up the day with a nice, big, panic attack inside of winding down and relaxing.

I found myself sitting on the edge of my couch one evening, bracing for the impact of another panic attack. I felt the "minty" feeling in my throat, my heart began to race as that suffocating feeling of doom crept in. Then, in a split-second, I glanced down at the floor and said to myself "Wait. I don't have to let this happen," and just like that, the panic was gone. I can't tell you where I put it or where it went, but as soon as I recognized I won in that instance, that I wasn't going to suffer for one second more than what I chose, that is when I began to feel hope again. I finally had control of this monster. I found my "grip" and never again would it blanket me in its sticky, menacing clutches. This was the start of many breakthroughs I had during this time.

It's hard to pinpoint exactly what caused this traumatic time in my life but I have a few theories. Jacquie, being a seasoned astrologer, informed me of the onerous Saturn Return that I was just coming out of and how it requires that we look at the last few years in our life and assess how well we'd done. If for any reason we think things didn't go well, we feel a stronger remorse and can either give up or, as in my case, rely on panic attacks to sidestep the things I could no longer avoid. It was also the year anniversary, almost to the day, that I had freed myself of the chains of an anti-depressant after six years of taking it. It could have been the death of Uncle Prep or even my sister going to jail and facing deportation back to England and me taking my nieces under my wing. It could have been living in an uninhabitable house with no heat and a landlord who refused to replace a broken furnace and having to find another home for my family of six before the city condemned our home. It may have been all of those reasons or maybe none at all, but regardless, this growth was meant to happen when it did and exactly as it did.

With this realization came the ability to revisit relationships in my life and let go of toxic people and events that had, unbeknownst to me, been shaping my life and feeding my anxiety. In letting go of these people and events, I was able to lose over 50 pounds of traumatic baggage from my body that I had been carrying around. My family and I found another home and moved in with the help of a few new friends. We also finally got custody of my stepdaughter after battling for over ten years.

One of my favorite mantras during this time was, "Crazy people don't think they're crazy," because for a while I was absolutely convinced that I was going off the deep end and that I would be taken away from my young family to live in an insane asylum for the rest of my life. I had to be told, "you are human," to understand. That was one of the most important bits of knowledge I had to hear and to finally absorb. Those three words spoken by Jacquie gave me the power of a thousand atomic power plants in the twinkling of an eye.

Looking back on all the times I had shrunk into myself because I allowed it was a revelation. My anxiety this time around was my attempt at coping with a series of unfortunate events; only this time, I was aware that it served me no good. Hindsight is 20/20, but at the time I was suffering I had no idea what I was allowing into my life. I was able to slowly control my anxiety by creating an empathic "shield" for myself; I told myself I deserved to be happy; I wrote my thoughts down both bad and good. I found "I am" statements particularly powerful (i.e., I *am* in control, I *am* safe). I wrapped myself in fluffy fleece blankets, spent days in my most comfortable pajamas, laid in bed watching silly videos with my toddler, and, most importantly, I laughed at myself. It took a while to get to the point where I could laugh at how ridiculous I was being in those first few moments of anxiety but now, it is so incredibly freeing.

I still have times of anxiety where I feel as though the air is too thin. When there is nothing else to be anxious about, my default, if nothing else, is breathing. I found a way to loosen the bands around my head and chest and move my mind to other thoughts. I can breathe, I can understand myself, I am whole and I have hope.

Flooding on New Year's Eve

by Melanie Green

I sat cross-legged on the sidewalk outside of my house in my long housedress. The dried tears made my face sticky. I thought about my choices and how they led me to the point I might lose my home due to slab leaks too costly to repair. I winced when I thought about how I might have been better prepared if I only kept the high-paying corporate job that bored me instead of pursuing a freelance writing career. Choices, I thought, unwilling to accept that sometimes things just happen.

I started to cry when I thought about all we'd lose, such as the money we invested in the house. Our homeowner's insurance policy was mediocre at best. We'd never get the money we'd need to fix it all. I questioned my career choices and wondered if I made huge mistakes for me and my family. I became a writer because I love writing, but it was taking much longer than I expected to make as much money as my regular job paid. I made a terrible mistake and now I couldn't fix it.

Staring at the concrete pavement I sat on, I ran my fingers across the cracked path. I thought about how there was nothing I could do if there were slab leaks like the plumber said there might be. What else could it be? I put my head on my knees. I'm going to lose everything.

Wiping away my tears, I walked back into the house and sat with my grandmother who was visiting us for New Year's Eve. She looked at me with an expression I couldn't quite recognize. It seemed like distrust mixed with fear. She looked at me for a moment before diverting her attention to the ground.

"I was thinking," she said. "I should take the train home tomorrow." She ruffled the blankets next to her on the couch.

"No," I told her. "Amtrak doesn't have anything scheduled tomorrow. You couldn't leave even if you wanted to."

"I don't want to be a bother." She looked around the living room, staring at the disassembled dishwasher and boxes of canned goods now residing in my living room.

Before she arrived, I scrubbed the floors and returned my usually cluttered home into its pristine state. I wanted her to be impressed by how great my home looked. Now, we sat waiting for the emergency plumber to come over and hoped he'd actually show even though it was now 10 p.m. on New Year's Eve.

I touched her shoulder and pulled her close to me. "I'm really glad you came up." I kissed her forehead.

I stood up and walked over to the now defrosting box of Cohen's hors d'oeuvres we spent a few hours looking for and the Korbel champagne we bought a few hours before we came home to find the house flooded.

"Pigs in a blanket and potato knishes?" I asked her.

"How can you cook them?" she asked with a look on her face that suggested she wasn't hungry but didn't want to deter my efforts either.

I hopped over the wet towels, saturated laminate flooring, and hoses into the kitchen to grab the toaster oven. I plugged it in near the couch and sat it on the coffee table. My husband walked in to the living room and stared at the toaster oven. He had wasted the last two hours futilely trying to save our bedroom's wooden floor. He knew the beautiful floors were one of the reasons I wanted to buy the house.

"Miniature weenies?" I asked him.

He laughed at me quietly and took some on a napkin. I poured three glasses of the champagne into three Solo cups left over from our Thanksgiving party. We ate in silence and waited for the plumber.

I turned on the TV. We only had a digital antennae, so our selection was shockingly limited. ABC's *Dick Clark's New Year's Rockin' Eve* aired, even though Dick Clark had died in 2012. Some rapper we didn't recognize performed songs we didn't know.

"I remember when this first premiered," my grandmother said. "It used to be my favorite." She smiled. "Your grandfather and I — when we lived in New York — we'd go to Times Square after we ate Chinese food."

"I feel that Chinese is kind of the tradition in the family," I said. She laughed. "It's the only place where they don't jack-up the prices. Plus, the pu pu platter at Ming's is the best. The first time we brought your…"

I stared at my grandmother and remembered why I first wanted to be a writer. She told me stories about old New York, of World War II, and what it was like to live in the 20th century. I loved listening to my grandmother's stories and saw so much value in them. I wanted to record such stories and really explore the human experience. I loved my grandmother and her stories.

This whole writing thing started in the fourth grade when she panicked about my future of lying. I used to tell such vivid stories about candy mountains and unicorns, she feared when I got older, I'd just make up crazy things. She handed me two five subject spiral notebooks and told me to write the stories in one and the truth in the other. I preferred the diary, where I could record what actually happened in my life. It was much better than fiction.

I rested my hand on my husband's knee and listened to my father's first time coming with my family to Ming's Chinese restaurant. Although the restaurant's been long closed, I know their egg rolls must have been truly spectacular. As a kid, my mom made my grandma bring them with her to Florida on the plane.

"Do you think it's safe to use the bathroom?" my grandmother asked. "With the plumbing and all?" She stood up.

"I'm sure it is," my husband said, as she walked down the hallway to the bathroom.

While she was out of hearing range, I held my husband's hand in my own. He looked as frazzled as I felt. "I've been thinking that it's just a house," I said.

"But it's our house," he said in a calmer tone than I'd expect from someone who punched a hole into a wall out of frustration earlier that evening.

"We can always get another one," I said. "This is what we can't replace. I know it didn't work out quite the way we thought, but Happy New Year, baby."

I kissed him quickly on the mouth.

My grandmother stood near us. "Should I go?"

I patted the couch. When she sat down, I pulled her toward me and kissed her cheek. "Happy New Year, Grandma. I love you."

"Happy New Year." After a brief hesitation, she said "Well, tomorrow can't be worse?"

The plumber knocked on the door. We got up instantly to open it and thanked him profusely for coming on New Year's Eve. We wanted him to know how much it meant to us. He was the only one who agreed to stop by. Every other plumber wanted to wait five days when they reopened after their offices were closed for the holiday. This would be a huge problem for us because the water kept flowing. Five days of this kind of flooding would certainly destroy our house.

My grandmother sat on the couch and sipped her champagne. She wasn't really supposed to have it, but I promised not to tell my mother. We showed the plumber the damage the flood caused so he'd know where to start. We started in the kitchen, the A/C closet, and then worked our way around the house. He even went with us outside to look at the A/C to make sure something wasn't wrong with how it was draining.

"I'm not an HVAC professional," the plumber said. "But I don't think it's your A/C system that's causing this kind of damage. Things look like they're draining there normally."

"That's a good thing in Florida," I said.

The plumber chuckled. "Well, sure. The bad news is that I'm not 100% sure where the leak is. From what I can tell from where the water traveled from the kitchen inside of this wall. I can't promise that, but it looks like it."

"Great, can you fix it?" my husband asked.

"That's the other thing," the plumber said. "I'm an emergency plumber, so I primarily work with leaky toilets and pipes, that type of thing. You need someone to confirm the leak and then go into the cinder block to fix it. This may or may not require the cabinets to come out."

I sighed deeply.

"There's good news here, though," he said. "First, it's not a slab leak. That's really important to say." He took out his phone from his pocket. "I'm going to give you two phone numbers."

My husband found a piece of paper and a pen.

"You call Eric tomorrow and tell him I told you to. He lives nearby and can confirm the location of the leak. Then, call Paul to come and fix it over the weekend. Also, I turned off the water to the kitchen so it won't leak anymore."

We thanked him and watched him leave. It was a good reminder of what matters and that even if we lost the house, we could rebuild.

And as my grandmother always said, at least it was something I could write about.

He's Got It Covered

by Debbie Day

It wasn't earth-shattering. It wasn't life or death. It certainly wasn't the worst thing I've had to deal with. But I guess that's why it amazed me so much. Yes, it was a small thing, but it mattered to me, so it mattered to Him too. That's what gave me hope.

I had just given birth to my twin boys only a few weeks before. In fact, I was driving on my way home from my six-week postpartum appointment when I grabbed a handful of beef jerky from the center console. As I took a bite, I felt a horrendous crunch. Something wasn't right. My tongue felt around for what had happened. Something bone-hard was floating around my mouth.

Have you ever had that icky dream where all your teeth fall out and you holler, "Noooo! Please let this be a dream!" Well, I had several of those nightmares long before the beef jerky incident, and every time I had woken up, I melted in relief knowing it hadn't been real. This time it was real.

My heart sunk when I realized which tooth was missing: the "cursed tooth." It was the one adjacent to my two front teeth. This tooth had given me problems my whole life. It had always been discolored and decayed. Not only that, but it had also been especially smaller than the surrounding teeth, so it stood out. Growing up, our large family didn't have a lot of money, and we couldn't afford to get it fixed, so I just tried to ignore it and move on with life.

After growing up and getting married, I finally got the "cursed tooth" fixed. It required an expensive root canal and a crown. After the procedure was complete, I was so surprised to see my smil; it actually looked normal. I may have shed a tear or two of happiness. It was just one of those small things I hoped would happen someday.

Well, now another day had come: the evil beef jerky reckoning day. I went straight my dentist's office. "Please just let this be a quick fix," I prayed.

Well, it wasn't going to be a quick fix. I was hoping the crown could simply be glued back on. However, it turns out that the underlying structure had become so brittle that the actual base had completely broken off. Apparently this is common after root canals. Who knew.

The dentist told me I would need a complicated surgery to screw an implant into my bone. He explained that the recovery would take at least four months, in which time I would need to be extremely careful with the implant site. I'd have to be on a special diet, and then after about six months (and several thousand dollars), I would have a new tooth.

I know I'm a wimp, but I'd like to think that postpartum hormones had to do with the drips I tried to keep from spilling out my eyes. The dentist grinned widely as if he was amused by my overreaction.

"Have you talked to a psychologist about post-partum depression?" he asked me.

"No, I'm just sensitive and it's a long story!" I blubbed.

Within a few minutes, he had glued a temporary tooth into place to last until I could get surgery and I went on my way.

After a couple months of getting second opinions and figuring out finances, I was sitting in the operating chair while the oral surgeon my dentist had recommended drilled the implant up into my facial bones. The surgery was complete. Now it was time for four months of eating a soft diet to allow the implant area to heal. During this time, I would need a temporary tooth placed in my mouth until I could get my final tooth.

Now, my oral surgeon was excellent at one thing: dental implant surgery. He was not however, excellent at dealing with prosthetic teeth. In fact, he informed me that he usually never placed teeth after surgery because his patients' dentist always did. But for some reason, my dentist didn't feel comfortable taking on the task. He said my case was too complicated.

"Well, since my dentist won't do it, can I have a different dentist be in charge of making my new tooth? Like, a cosmetic dentist?" I asked the surgeon.

"You are a difficult case. I don't want anyone ruining the work I've done. I need to do it," he told me. So my surgeon put in my temporary tooth. And thus began a unique season of my life. The season of my tooth falling out over and over again.

This is how it would happen: The oral surgeon would put the temporary tooth in. I would go home and several hours later, without warning, the tooth popped off. There were two requirements to these incidents: number one was that it had to happen after the office was closed, and number two was that when I did get ahold of the office, they had to schedule my appointment for the smack-dab middle of the day when I'd need a babysitter in order to come in.

I can't even count the number of times that temporary tooth fell off. I was constantly worried that at any moment I'd turn into gap-toothed pirate lady. Then there was the reoccurring stress of finding a babysitter to once again watch the twins while I drove to the office. On several occasions, my husband even had to come home from work and use his vacation time so I could get it taken care of.

Finally, after months of anxiety, it was time to get the final tooth placed. The surgeon assured me this tooth should last ten years — possibly even a lifetime — but of course, I was a little worried.

A part of me wasn't even surprised when it came loose the very next day. That's the moment when I lost all hope. I was officially convinced there would never be a solution to my tooth fiasco. The thing really was cursed.

On the drive back to the office to get it re-cemented for the thirtieth time, I began to pray. I admit it. I cried while I prayed. (Can you tell yet that I'm a crier?)

"What do I do?" I asked God. "Do I trust that my surgeon will get it right eventually? Do I go to a different doctor even though he insisted *he* had to do it? I just don't want to forever be afraid that at any moment, one of my front teeth will fall out!"

I came to a stop light just blocks away from the office. I was sniffling up my tears and had just finished dumping all my complaints and concerns to God when I suddenly noticed the car in front of me. I couldn't believe what I saw.

The license plate directly ahead had the following saying around the border: "God's got it covered." And then to my utter disbelief, the license plate itself read: "UR SMILE."

I couldn't help but laugh. "Really, God? Wow."

That small message was exactly what I needed in that moment. Instantly, I felt renewed hope. Now I knew that the creator of the universe actually cared about my silly little tooth problem, and without a doubt, He "had it covered."

I got the permanent tooth placed again, and this time it actually stayed in. After a while, I began to think that maybe my curse was finally lifted. Then about nine months later, I was playing with my toddler and his head unexpectedly bumped into my face. I felt a terrible crunch.

You've got to be kidding me.

I went back to the surgeon and discovered the expensive crown as well as the abutment underneath were completely broken. He told me he'd have to entirely remake them, costing me thousands of dollars more. I was angry, frustrated, and didn't know what to do. My only hope came from remembering God's promise a year ago. "He's got it covered."

Through a series of prayers and miracles, the oral surgeon offered to refund me the money for the first crown and abutment so I could afford to have it redone with someone else.

I did lots of research and found a well-reviewed dentist in town who agreed to do the procedure at a great price.

"This is it!" I thought. "This will be my solution!"

Well, just days later, my husband landed a new job 2,000 miles away in a small town in the middle of Wyoming (a.k.a. nowhere). The employer wanted him to start immediately. That meant we had only three weeks to get my tooth fixed. (I certainly wasn't counting on anyone in Smalltown, Wyoming being able to help me.)

My new dentist tried his best, he really did. But the permanent crown looked so bad. Even he agreed. And there just wasn't any time to get it right before we had to leave.

"Why isn't this working out?" I wondered. I felt so doubtful and afraid. Again, I remembered God's promise from so long ago. It was my only source of hope.

The new dentist didn't charge me a dime for at least trying to fix my tooth, which I was grateful for. And just like that, we moved across the country and I began to research local dentists once again. That's when I found Dr. Smiley. As it turns out, Dr. Smiley from Nowheretown was the best dentist I'd been to yet. Go figure.

The solution didn't come immediately. With the shape of my mouth and gums, I really was a difficult case. But finally after four months (and the birth of our third child, a girl!), Dr. Smiley was able to fix the cursed tooth. Not only that, but he also provided simple procedures that, along with a new permanent crown, improved my overall smile in ways I didn't even know were possible; something no other dentist had ever offered in the past. It was a miracle!

It was three years from the infamous beef jerky day to the day my tooth was finally fixed for good. What I learned in that time was that we need never lose hope. Why? Because God cares about even our smallest of struggles, and even though we may doubt at times, He always keeps His promises. He's got it covered.

Déjà Vu

By Georgia A. Hubley

I remember the summer I was six-years-old, and my friends and I counted down the days until school would start in the fall. Unbeknownst to me, my parents were making other plans.

I was too young to understand the country's economy was in a slump and my folks were barely making ends meet. They'd made the decision to move to a farm in rural central Ohio to save money.

There'd been whispers behind closed doors, then one morning at breakfast the words were loud and clear, "We're moving to the country and must sell what we don't need," Mom said. "We're only taking the barest of necessities with us."

A week later, a Call the Junk Man truck appeared and almost all of our dishes, pots, pans, clothing and furnit,ure were loaded into his vehicle. Waves of sadness washed over me as I watched tears stream down Mom's face while the junk man counted the cash for our belongings into Dad's hand.

The next morning, our remaining possessions were packed into boxes and loaded into a moving van, along with our remaining furniture.

"Make sure you haven't left anything behind," Dad said to Mom, my four-year-old brother, and me, before we got into the car and followed the moving van to the farm.

The seventy miles to our destination was a long and tiring trip, but to help pass the time, we all joined in and played I Spy and sang silly songs. The final five mile stretch was a dicey ride as Dad navigated the car over the narrow, winding, rough gravel road that lead to our farm.

When Dad pulled into the lane leading to the farmhouse, Mom turned to my brother and me in the backseat, "I want you to remember, roughing-it builds character. Life is a grand adventure."

I soon discovered our new home was a 100-year-old, drafty farmhouse without the modern conveniences of electricity, a telephone, or indoor plumbing.

The grand adventure began with battling wasps that had made a nest inside the outhouse, which was secluded in a patch of pink and red hollyhocks.

"Wasps are as afraid of you as you are of them," Mom said. I didn't want to test her theory.

At dusk, Mom taught me to light the four kerosene lamps needed to provide light for each room. Later, I'd learn how to stoke a fire and keep it going in the coal-burning stove that heated the entire farmhouse. I marveled at how Mom prepared a meal on a wood-burning stove located in the corner of the kitchen, and that there was hot water waiting in the side reservoir of that wood-stove.

After a meal, I ladled hot water from the reservoir into a dishpan so Mom could wash the dishes. I perched myself on a tall, wobbly, red wooden stool, dried the dishes and whined about us now living miles from nowhere. My six-year-old mindset pondered how the school bus would find me so I could begin school the day after Labor Day. Mom assured me that together, we'd walk the 250 yards to the end of the lane and she'd flag down the school bus.

It didn't take long to adapt to our new rural life. We all made new friends. Mom and Dad worked hard at making a living on the farm. Over a span of five years, electricity and a telephone were installed in the old farmhouse, and a gas range replaced Mom's wood cooking stove. However, the outhouse remained a permanent fixture.

My childhood was a happy one in spite of the hardships. Indeed, I learned to rough it. Life on the farm prepared me to be launched into adulthood and to leave the nest. Eventually, I married and had a family of my own. Live was grand.

Flash forward: Our two sons learned to fly and our nest is empty. However, retirement income isn't as plentiful as my husband and I thought it'd be. Downsizing is on the horizon.

I have a déjà vu moment: I'm that little girl watching Mom pare down her life and sell the family's worldly goods. Can I be as brave as Mom?

"Move" and "pack" are four-letter words. Moving day looms. The buyers for our house requested a 30-day occupancy date and we agreed to their terms, besides selling our house at a loss.

There's one week left to sort, toss, donate, pack, and move. I try to ignore the twinge of uneasiness in the pit of my stomach. How can I part with so many cherished things?

I've saved the kitchen for last. I fight back tears as I make certain the kitchen cabinets and drawers are empty and everything is placed on the countertops for sorting. The stark reality is I must decide which items I really need, not what I want to keep for sentimental reasons. My new kitchen is one-third the size of the one I'm leaving behind.

A surge of melancholy races through me while I fill box after box of donations for charitable organizations. My eyes well up with tears, because there are too many memories attached to the two dozen un-matched coffee mugs that must go. There's a tug at my heart strings, as I wrap each mug in bubble wrap.

Negotiating with the bank and selling our house at a loss was upsetting but necessary. Fortunately, after a two-month search, we found a small condo within walking distance to shops, businesses, and eateries. It's finally possible to be a one-car family.

Excitement ensues on moving day, until the professional movers arrive with our furniture. The first piece of furniture they unload is the beautiful oak desk that matches my computer hutch, lateral file, and bookcase. For weeks, I've envisioned these stunning oak pieces in the small bedroom we've chosen for my new office. Regretfully, my vintage desk won't fit and it must go.

As our move-in progresses, every nook and cranny is filled and it is apparent more paring-down is necessary. I'm unable to choke back the tears as favorite items are exiled to the garage.

Do we sell or donate the leftover furniture? It's too crowded to park our car in the garage and my husband doesn't have access to his work-bench.

I'm relieved the movers are gone; time to relax, celebrate, and toast to our new abode.

Suddenly, I hear my husband laughing uproariously and loud voices coming from the garage.

I'm dumbstruck. Neighbors galore are mingling in our garage. "I literally had a garage sale," my husband chuckles. "I sold everything."
After the garage sale we reflect on the day's events, as my husband opens a bottle of wine and fills two wine glasses.

I gaze about our new kitchen. That déjà vu moment and a tinge of guilt engulfs my senses as I recall Mom coping with the hardships of downsizing to an old farmhouse without the comforts I take for grant-ed. How grateful I am for our modern new digs. I gather my thoughts and composure and make a toast, "To creating happy memories within these new walls, and to having indoor plumbing."

One Door Closes — Reality Knocks Twice

by Gayle Redfern

One day, many years ago, as I drove home from a stressful corporate day, the following words popped into my head: You will never return to this business; the door has closed.

Immediately, I thought about this life pattern with fright. My husband was taking courses leading to a new career and I had the only income. How could I, the perfectly organized person, solve all life's problems with no job, no income?

All my life I had pushed away my spirit thoughts simply because they did not fit into the corporate world, or follow the teachings of my parents; they were unacceptable. I had spent all this time trying to conform to everybody, following family and society rules. Now this door slammed shut, pushing me into an unknown world. I bounced from one accepted way of thinking to a questionable one. Now I was asking myself: How could I live the proper life if I walked away from, and rejected, the social expectations?

After this extremely stressful drive home from the office, I phoned my boss and said "no more." The corporate bosses gave me three choices: take heavy drugs, go into a mental hospital, or see a psychiatrist. The first two went completely against my values and even though I had a Psych degree, I rejected the thought of seeing a psychiatrist. None of these conformed to my corporate perspective, nor did they conform to my social values.

My life became a roller-coaster, searching for an acceptable path that could make me happy, win the approval of family and friends, all while living in a corporate maze. For many years since I was a child, I had felt approval was more important than my happiness. Now I wanted to stand on a street corner and shout. But this too was unacceptable. I was in a strange world, with no love, no acceptance; what could I do.

Fortunately, my spirit guides led me away from the three political choices. However, this only reinforced the thought that the closed door had pushed me into limbo for a reason. What was I going to do now?

I was living in secluded, isolated thinking, unsure of what to do, and had done so for many years. I knew I needed people around me but didn't know where to find them, or how to build a social circle. I did not realize how much I depended upon networks stemming from the work world.

Corporate clubs and community breakfast meetings were no long available. I didn't even know what my interests were any more, what was allowed. This led to heavy depression. When the one door had closed and I discovered my spirit friends were sitting patiently waiting to open at least one more.

Unless someone has experienced this isolation, they cannot say, "I understand," with total integrity.

These people realize there are a number of avenues leading to the ideal reality bang on the door. They will also realize there is usually more than one solution; a key is discovering the optimum one. Listen to spirit friends, or to your instinct.

When a door shuts, it is prudent to look for alternatives. Doors in our lives always shut for a reason. Begin by putting a sign in your home: "One door has closed to give me the key to my reality."

A shutting door in your life provides several options. I have met various people who were "forced" into specific careers that did not meet their desires. After intentionally slamming doors in personal lives, they finally listened to their spirit friends and became successful in following individual goals.

Once the shock is over, it is important to understand that there are options. Our spirit friends will guide us but we still have to work. It is up to the individual to decide which knock might lead to hope and a golden opportunity.

Depression is not easy to get rid of but it is possible. I knew I needed people around but was cautious as to their intent, so at first I just looked for strangers. This did not help. Consequently, I began taking these actions.

First, I asked myself: How much time in my life have I struggled to conform? Did I struggle in denial, blocking the information that my family and society kept pushing upon me. Did I consider the information as unexplained and illogical norms; all I really want to do is

---

Second, I wrote down what I felt my values are and how they contribute to the healing of people, society and the planet. It is surprising how connected they are.

Third, I began the proverbial bucket list. This helps determine the importance of your values.

For those unfamiliar with the expression "bucket list," it represents the number of experiences or achievements that a person hopes to have, or accomplish, during their lifetime. This phrase became popular through the movie *Bucket List* from 2007, starring Jack Nicholson and Morgan Freeman.

The items from a bucket list, as well as highlighting personal values, lead to possible activities. For example, one of my interests was learning more about alternate healing and application. Since I didn't know what to do, I took time to study specific fields of healing, leading to a Master of Arts in Holistic Health.

My thesis reviewed seven international health care systems available in North America. As I reviewed each method, I looked at the probability of opening a clinic out of our home and including specific modalities. My husband and I were looking for a new home; this was added to the list of requirements.

Fourth, gather groups of like-minded people. This is perhaps one of the most import actions. However, until I was able to sort out and answer "Who I am," I was unable to find the special compatible companions. I learned that one of the important ways to open a closed door is surrounding yourself with positive individuals. These are key steps:

Prove them wrong by searching out individuals who were already in business field.

Bookstores selling corresponding topics will contribute a matching audience.

Evening or weekend courses also provide like-minded groups.
As friends and family offer support for depression, they inadvertently shed negative thoughts. This was my narrow world. The words, I heard, "won't work," or "not done in this region," or "you're too old," are only a few comments thrown at me.

I began getting to know the people and the products of a metaphysical bookstore. Through this extension, I surrounded myself with a wondrous group of friends of similar interests, building and strengthening the spirit communication.

This group encouraged us to open the clinic and helped us begin advertising. It was a slow start but looked positive. The clinic included powerful therapeutic techniques to heal a variety of individuals. Our social and spiritual group expanded to include alternative healing merging with spirit healing. I was able to share the spirit messages through readings at our clinic. This combined both major reality knocks.

I finally thought I was on the right path; I walked through a door that was previously closed and was finally confident that the door of reality was gifting me my life purpose, healing, and spirit messaging.

Then one day during a peaceful meditation, I received another message: leave the healing to others, write books instead that includes our message. This way each individual gets the information they need.

I was stunned. I trusted my spirit information but still had reservations based upon years of social programming.

I started on a whirlwind depression and struggled to climb out. I finally understood that this was the second reality knock.

First I was told "Trust us." I received a detail book: *Inner Bridges*.

Then I was told "We will help you." I received the titles and sections of a book: *Within & Beyond*.

Finally, they said: "You know how to write, we will guide you toward the people who need the most help." *Ancient Wisdoms, Exploring the Mysteries and Connection* was born. My spirits nudged me toward cultures around the world. As soon as it was published, the next message was: "There is a need for a follow-up; this has only piqued the curiosity."

Currently, I am working on *Ancient Wisdoms II, Many Corners, Many Voices*.

As I look back over my lifetime and the depressions I've endured I realize that although more than one door has closed over the years, the biggest one with a loudest bang threw me out of the corporate world. It taught me lessons similar to those of many other individuals.

Take time to learn that you have control over the reality you encounter, and it approaches you with gentleness and love. No matter what troubles you bump into, reality always carries the hope we find.

Each soul comes to earth with a definite purpose, linking many lives or spirits. I now realize that life closes many doors and it is our opportunity to maximize the chances that life gives us.

For my awareness, reality knocked twice but I have heard three responses, merging the knowledge I have. First, I heal when my spirit friends tell me someone needs it. Second, I will pass on specific information through a spirit reading, if I am told it is acceptable. And lastly, the main focus is writing publications which spread the spirit wisdom to those who need pertinent topics.

If your feel there is no hope, then pause and follow the guidelines and enjoy the reality.

When one door closes, reality knocks twice.

Contributors
(in order that their article appears)

MARYBETH MITCHAM holds a MPH in nutrition and works as a professor and a nutrition and healthy living educator. She is an Adirondack 46er, motorcycle rider, pianist, and published freelance author who, when not working, can be found hiking, hovering by the wood stove, digging a pond, or at marybeth.mitcham@gmail.com.

A.C. GRAHAM aspires to be a full-time, successful writer. Until then, he is stuck with a boring 9-to-5 job to pay the bills. He has been blessed with an awesome partner after kissing countless frogs for years. You may find out more about him at alcasgraham.blogspot.co.id

TRISHA MAHI is an evidential medium who now limits her practice to match her limited available time on her coffee and macadamia nut farm in Hawaii. She still speaks with a few word-of-mouth clients, and writes for *New Spirit Journal* when the angels tap her on the shoulder. Learn more at www.ihearangels.com.

FRANCINE BILLINGSLEA says, "I am finding my new niche and passion for writing in my latter years, I have been published in more than 45 publications. I am a breast cancer survivor and a "Jersey girl" who lives in the Atlanta area. I love to write, travel, and spend quality time with my family and loved ones."

NIOBE WEAVER shares her gifts of healing through her voice. She is a visionary speaker, channel, sound healer, and mystic. A near death experience opened Niobe to her mission of soul reflection. This sonic in-body experience of your beauty awakens and reveals the purpose of your soul. Learn more about Niobe at www.niobeweaver.com

MAUREEN GILBERT is a certified bioenergetic therapist, life coach, and ordained dinister. She is a true global nomad, having lived and worked in eight countries. Maureen loves helping people with transformation. She is unique in her ability to link both the deeply spiritual with the profoundly practical. She blogs on spirituality and personal transformation on her websites: LoveAndFinances.com and TrulySeen.com.

LISA ROMEO is a New Jersey writer, editor, and writing professor. Her work is a Notable in Best American Essays 2016; has been nominated for a Pushcart; and published widely, including the *New York Times*, *O The Oprah Magazine*, *Brevity*, *The Manifest Station*, and several essay anthologies. Her blog, http://LisaRomeo.blogspot.com, offers resources and advice for writers. Connect on Twitter: @LisaRomeo.

JANEL GRADOWSKI lives in a land that looks like a cold weather clothing accessory, the mitten-shaped state of Michigan. She is a wife and mom to two kids plus one Golden Retriever. Her stories have appeared in many publications, both online and in print. She is also the author of The Culinary Competition Mystery Series. Her website is www.JanelGradowski.com.

ASHLEY H is an aspiring writer and poet who is currently working towards her B.A. degree in sociology and English. Ever since she was a girl she has dreamed of becoming a writer. She has mostly written poetry, but has recently started to work on both fiction and nonfiction articles and stories. Some of her poetry can be read at wordsaregolden22.tumblr.com

BEAR KOSIK has authored novels, plays, short fiction, essays, poetry, and a nonfiction book on democracy in the USA. Bear's third novel was published late in 2016 by Double Dragon Press. Four short plays appeared Off-Off-Broadway in 2016. He has author profiles on Amazon, GoodReads, and Smashwords. Bear also designs notecards and t-shirts available at www.bearlydesigned.com.

LISA BRAXTON earned her M.F.A. in creative writing from Southern New Hampshire University and her M.S. in journalism from Northwestern University. She is former president of the Boston chapter of the Women's National Book Association. Her stories have appeared in literary journals and anthologies. She has completed a novel, which she hopes to get published. Her website is www.lisabraxton.com.

CLARA FREEMAN is a freelance writer and motivational author. A former nurse who loves being a mom, grandma, and recent great-grandma, she uses her life experiences to inspire and encourage others. A *Huffington Post* contributor, Clara is awaiting release of her inspirational book, *Unleash Your Pearls Empowering Women Voices*. Visit Clara's blog site at http://wisewoman2.wordpress.com

DARRELL GILKES is a recently graduated teacher residing in Newmarket, Ontario, Canada. Though he has cerebral palsy, he doesn't let that get in the way of what he wants to achieve. He has a passion for writing in the hopes that one day he might get his own book released. You can contact him at darrell.gilkes@hotmail.com

DIANA RAAB, Ph.D. is an award-winning memoirist, poet, and blogger who advocates the healing and transformative powers of writing. She's the author of eight books, and gives nationwide writing workshops. Her book, *Writing for Bliss: Telling Your Story and Transforming Your Life* is due out in the Fall of 2017. She's a regular blogger for *Psychology Today* and the *Huffington Post*.

NANCY LYNN WHITE is a freelance writer and a graduate of Capital University in Columbus, Ohio with a B.A. in English/technical writing. She is a member of the Scribophile Critique Group. Her craft memberships include Romance Writers of America (PRO member), Central Ohio Fiction Writers, and The Writer's Center. Publications: "The Boss From Hell," *Work Literary* Magazine, 12/1/14; "You're Safer in a Plane, Than in a Car," *Shatter the Looking Glass* Magazine, 1/1/15; "Children Should be Seen, Not Heard," *Only Trollops Shave Above the Knee* anthology, Blue Lobster Book Co., May 2015; "Sippin' Bourbon Dressing," *Good Old Days* magazine, December 2016 and "True Love Never Dies," *The Narcicisst's Playbook* anthology, Spring 2017. Currently, she is working on her first novel.

ELIZABETH PHILIP resides in the Midwest with her husband, two children, and three spoiled dogs. When away from her keyboard, she enjoys reading, cooking, and spending time in the Smoky Mountains. Her essays have appeared in various anthologies.

JACQUELINE SEEWALD has taught creative, expository, and technical writing at Rutgers University as well as high school English. She also worked as both an academic librarian and an educational media specialist. Sixteen of her books of fiction have been published to critical praise including books for adults, teens, and children. Her short stories, poems, essays, reviews, and articles have appeared in hundreds of diverse publications and numerous anthologies such as: *The Writer*, *L.A. Times*, *Reader's Digest*, *Pedestal*, *Sherlock Holmes Mystery Magazine*, *Gumshoe Review*, *Library Journal*, *The Christian Science Monitor*, and *Publishers Weekly*. Her writer's blog can be found at http://jacquelineseewald.blogspot.com

PATTY SOMLO's most recent books are *The First to Disappear* (Spuyten Duyvil), a Finalist in the 2016 International Book Awards, and *Even When Trapped Behind Clouds: A Memoir of Quiet Grace* (WiDo Publishing). She has received four Pushcart Prize nominations, one for storySouth Million Writers Award, and had an essay selected as Notable for Best American Essays 2014. www.pattysomlo.com.

AVERY STILEs is an emerging author in the heart of Phoenix, Arizona. Her work is primarily Young Adult to New Adult, featuring themes inspired by science fiction, fantasy, and anything in-between. Contact Avery at averyjstiles@gmail.com, and find more information at averystiles.com.

AMY LAI, M.D. graduated from Harvard a College and Harvard Medical School. She lives in Indiana with her husband and children.

LISA LIPSCOMB is a mother, grandmother, public school teacher, instructional designer, nature lover, writer, and poet. She is the author of *Somewhere in the Middle of Love* and a self-professed life-long learner. Visit her website/blog at http://lisalipscombinharmony.blogspot.com/ or contact her via email at LisaLipscomb313@gmail.com

MICHELLE CHALKEY is a freelance writer based in Des Moines, IA. Specializing in health and lifestyle topics, Michelle blogs for businesses and writes magazine articles. Michelle also writes about self-development and stress management on her website, www.michellechalkey.com. When she is not reading or writing, Michelle and her husband are likely getting sushi or walking the dog.

Contact Michelle via email: mchalkey@gmail.com.

S.K. NAUS says she has enjoyed writing since grade school. She writes, "I love arranging words in the right order to create wonderful stories, and that's my favorite part of writing. I currently work in the secretarial field."

RUTH J. HARTMAN is a published author of over twenty books consisting of mysteries, contemporary and historical romance, a children's book and a memoir. She and her husband of 34 years live in rural Indiana with three very spoiled cats. The cats don't have an online presence. However, you can read more about Ruth's books at her website: www.ruthjhartman.blogspot.com.

BEATRICE M. HOGG is a writer and social worker in Sacramento, CA. She has a B.A. in social work from the University of Pittsburgh and a M.F.A. in creative writing from Antioch University Los Angeles. From 2008 to 2015, she experienced long-term unemployment and homelessness. She has a blog at www.marvellaland.wordpress.com and can be reached at HoggPen57@yahoo.com.

ROBYN ALEZANDERS is a freelance writer who always thinks about glitter, faeries, and dancing in the rain, because every day is now filled with happiness. Her work has appeared in print in *Nemonymous 5*, and *The Mammoth Book of the Kama Sutra*, and online at Eternal Haunted Summer. Find her on Facebook, where posts include pix of homemade vegan goodies.

KYRA SIDWELL-HARSH is a wife and mother living with her family in eastern Pennsylvania. Kyra came to America from England with her family as a child and attended schools in Pennsylvania. She has loved writing her entire life, is an accomplished artist, numerologist, activist, and spiritual blogger. Kyra aspires to be an author and art therapist. Visit her blog at www.starzkarmickyra.wordpress.com or contact her by email at kyraanne@live.com

MELANIE GREEN is a freelance writer and editor living in Tampa, Florida. She loves to edit novels, write short form articles, and create screenplays. She earned her M.F.A. in creative writing from National University and her B.A. in writing from the University of Tampa. You can find out more about her at www.melaniegreen.info.

DEBBIE DAY has always been passionate about writing stories that uplift. While she has a special interest in children's literature, she finds joy in any writing project. She published her first children's book, *Itchy Mitchie* in March 2015. Her inspiration comes from her Christian faith, family, and love of adventure. Follow her at debbiedayauthor.blogspot.com or on her Facebook page, DebbieDay Creations.

GEORGIA A. HUBLEY retired after 20 years from the money world to write about her world. Her stories appear in various anthologies and magazines. Once the nest was empty, Georgia and her husband of 38 years left California's Silicon Valley and relocated to the Nevada desert. Visit her website: www.georgiahubley.com

GAYLE REDFERN's passion is sharing her lifelong interest in spirituality, holistic and alternative health. She spends her time writing books and lecturing, sharing her passion for ancient teachings led by spirit messages and keeping her website, www.livingwholistically. com, alive. Living wholistically leads to good health and happiness. It involves the physical body, and the mental and spiritual aspects of our life. Contact Gayle at livingwholistically.com

Proof

Made in the USA
Charleston, SC
08 March 2017